RUNNING UP THE ST

# Francis W. Dixon

## RUNNING
## UP THE STAIRS

*Words of Life Paperback No. 2*

LAKELAND
MARSHALL, MORGAN & SCOTT
116 Baker Street,
LONDON W1M 2BB

Copyright © Francis W. Dixon 1975
First published 1975
ISBN 0 551 00578 5

Printed in Great Britain by Cox & Wyman Ltd,
London, Reading and Fakenham

# Contents

# Introduction

The title of this book may appear to be unusual, and it therefore calls for a word of explanation. I am well aware of the apostle's testimony when he said: "We preach not ourselves, but Christ Jesus the Lord; and ourselves your servants for Jesus' sake" (2 Cor. 4:5); and I always want this to be my testimony as well. At the same time, my Bournemouth friends, and many thousands of others who have visited our church over the years, will recognise the significance of this title.

The stairs referred to are those of our Lansdowne pulpit, and strangely enough, over these nearly three decades, I have never found it easy to walk up them sedately. The alternative has been to break into a run! Perhaps this unconscious habit is somehow connected with the muscles controlling my legs and feet; but, in all seriousness, there is another reason. Every preacher has his own eccentricities, but, allowing for that, I can truthfully say that as the time has drawn near for preaching I have always been eager to run into the pulpit and get going.

Some years ago, two people, who afterwards became my close friends, came to our church for the first time. When I went up into the pulpit, one turned to the other and said, "Did you see that? He *ran* up into the pulpit!" Also, at regular intervals, I hear from a friend who always begins or ends his letter with the question: "Are you still running up the stairs?" Then, just recently, I met one of God's prayer warriors, and she said, "Mr Dixon, whenever I attended your church I always waited for the door to open so that I could watch you come in and run up into the pulpit! I felt that you meant business, and that you were eager to start preaching the Word."

I hope my readers will accept this explanation of the reason for my choosing the title *Running up the Stairs,* and that they will catch a glimpse of the significance of this from the first sermon-study in the book. I pray that many will find encouragement, inspiration, instruction and help from these pages, and that those who preach the Word may wish to use some of the material for the furtherance of the gospel.

"Let us run . . . looking unto Jesus" (Heb. 12: 1–2).

F.W.D.

Bournemouth, England. 1975

# 1 : A Preacher
# in a Hurry

*And the angel of the Lord spake unto Philip,
saying, Arise, and go toward the south unto
the way that goeth down from Jerusalem unto
Gaza, which is desert. And he arose and went:
and, behold, a man of Ethiopia, an eunuch of
great authority under Candace queen of the
Ethiopians, who had the charge of all her
treasure, and had come to Jerusalem for to
worship, was returning, and sitting in his
chariot read Esaias the prophet. Then the
Spirit said unto Philip, Go near, and join
thyself to this chariot. And Philip ran thither
to him . . . (Acts 8: 26–30)*

This eighth chapter of Acts is packed full of movement.
The chief character is Philip, of whom we first read
in chapter 6, where we are told that he and six other men
were chosen to "serve tables" (Acts 6: 2–5). In the latter
part of this chapter and throughout chapter 7, we have the
record of Stephen's preaching, his courageous defence
before the authorities, and his martyrdom. Then, as we
come into chapter 8, it is Philip who is brought before us,
and it would seem that when Stephen was taken out of
the picture, Philip took his place. In the earlier part of
the chapter we see him preaching to great crowds in
Samaria, where souls were saved, lives were transformed
and many sick and afflicted people were healed. Then, at
the height of his success, having been the instrument in
God's hands in bringing great joy to the whole region of
Samaria, he was called away to take the gospel to one
man.

I want to introduce Philip to you as a preacher in a
hurry, for in Acts 8: 30 we read: *"And Philip ran . . ."*
Under the direct leading of the Holy Spirit, and in
humble obedience to God, he had come a hundred miles,

as he travelled from Samaria to the Gaza Desert, where there was in all probability a posting station en route from Jerusalem, and then down south across the desert. Philip was journeying under sealed orders, and he must have wondered what God's purpose was in taking him away from the crowded congregations and leading him, like Abraham, "not knowing whither he went" (Heb. 11: 8). Suddenly, however, he became aware of at least one very important reason why the Lord had brought him this way, for in front of him he saw a man of Ethiopia; he was sitting in his chariot and he was reading a scroll, which Philip afterwards discovered was part of Isaiah's prophecy. It was then that "the Spirit said unto Philip, Go near, and join thyself to this chariot. And Philip ran thither to him . . ." (Acts 8: 30). Yes, he ran! This preacher ran; he was in a hurry. Why did he run? Why was he in such a hurry?

Bishop Taylor Smith had a novel answer to that question. He used to say, "Of course Philip ran! If he hadn't done so, he would have lost his text!" By this, of course, he meant that if Philip had delayed, by then the queen's treasurer would have read well past Isaiah, chapter 53, and would have been reading from Isaiah 54! Well, that is perfectly true; but I want to suggest some other answers implied in the statement that "Philip ran . . ." because surely every preacher, every servant of the Lord, every evangelist and every soul-winner should run on the King's business. What may we safely deduce from the fact that "Philip ran . . ."?

(1) *Philip ran because God had told him to do something, and he was ready and eager to do it.*

This is beautifully brought out here; notice that when "the angel of the Lord spake unto Philip, saying, Arise, and go . . .", we read that Philip "arose and went" (verses 26 and 27). Notice again that when "the Spirit said unto Philip, Go near, and join thyself to this chariot . . ." we are told that "Philip ran thither to him . . ." (verses 29 and 30). Here is a clear indication of instant, unquestioning

10

obedience. Here was a man who was available to the Lord, ready for anything and prompt in his response to divine leading. Not only had Philip obeyed the Lord in leaving Samaria for what was to him an unknown destination, but now, when he was in the desert receiving further instructions, his obedience was prompt and complete. Philip could have said with the psalmist: "I will *run* the way of Thy commandments" (Ps. 119: 32); in other words, "I will always be ready to obey the Lord, and to say with David's men of old: 'Thy servants are ready to do whatsoever my lord the king shall appoint.'" (2 Sam. 15: 15.)

This is the kind of man whom God can use: a man who is available to Him and whom He can trust to obey Him without questioning; a man who, like Philip, is sensitive enough to hear His voice and to receive directions from Heaven; and a man who has enough faith to reckon on the fact that God knows what He is doing!

One of the first qualifications for usefulness in the service of God, whether that service is in the form of preaching to the crowd or witnessing to an individual, taking a Sunday school class or visiting the sick, is a readiness, an alacrity to obey God. We must be able to say, as Jesus, in the voice of prophecy, said: "I delight to do Thy will, O My God: yea, Thy law is within My heart" (Ps. 40: 8). How eager Philip was to do God's will; he *ran* to obey Him!

(2) *Philip ran because he had been entrusted with the gospel, and he was ready and eager to share it.*

If we move on in the Book of Acts to chapter 21, thereby covering a period of twenty years, we find there that he is described as "Philip the evangelist" (Acts 21: 8). That is what he was; he was a man sent by God to tell others about the Saviour; he was a man commissioned to preach the gospel, and he was eager to do it. But in the same manner, we have been commissioned to evangelise the lost and to tell others of our wonderful Saviour and Lord. Indeed, we are trustees of the gospel

11

and, like Paul, we can say: "we were allowed of God to be put in trust with the gospel" (1 Thess. 2: 4).

You see, God has given us a very wonderful gift. He has given His own dear Son to be our Saviour; but in giving us His Son He has said to us: "Now, don't keep Him to yourself! Share Him with everybody else!" – "Go ye into all the world, and preach the gospel to every creature" (Mark 16:15). Are we doing it? Or are we keeping this wonderful gift to ourselves? Philip was eager to tell others, and we see him *running* to do it.

In Matthew 28: 5–8, there is a beautiful picture brought before us; notice the words in *italics*: "And the angel answered and said unto the women, Fear not ye: for I know that ye seek Jesus, which was crucified. He is not here: for He is risen, as He said. Come, see the place where the Lord lay. And *go quickly, and tell* His disciples that He is risen from the dead; and, behold, He goeth before you into Galilee; there shall ye see Him: lo, I have told you. *And they departed quickly* from the sepulchre with fear and with great joy; *and did run* to bring His disciples word." Why did the women run? They ran because their Lord and Saviour had risen! They had expected to find Him in the tomb, but the angel had told them that He had risen from the dead, so they went quickly to tell the others that the Lord was alive! Surely, we would have done the same – or would we? Do we do less today? We ought to be able to say, with Paul: "I am debtor ..." (Rom. 1:14); "I am in debt to others to give them the gospel. I owe them the gospel."

(3) *Philip ran because the business in which he was engaged was urgent; it was a matter of life and death.*

How wonderfully God "caused both ends to meet" in bringing Philip and the queen's treasurer together at the precise moment when the one could be of help to the other! If Philip had not been quick to obey, this Ethiopian and all his followers might well have driven off into the desert, and it would have been impossible to make contact with them. But it was all in the plan and purpose of God that he should meet Philip, and Philip did not fail Him. This also reminds us of the urgency of our task, for there is no time to be lost in the matter of bringing the gospel to those who are without Christ. Like our Lord and Master, we should say: "I must work the works of Him that sent Me, while it is day: the night cometh, when no man can work" (John 9: 4); and like the great apostle Paul, we should say: "For though I preach the gospel, I have nothing to glory of: for necessity is laid upon me; yea, woe is unto me, if I preach not the gospel!" (1 Cor. 9: 16) We are living now in the day of grace, but we must not forget that this will soon end; then will be ushered in the day of judgment. This is why the King's business requires haste (1 Sam. 21: 8). People around us are dying, without God and without hope. How wonderful it would be if we could emulate Paul in his great compassion for the souls of men! For you will remember that in his closing speech to the elders at Ephesus, he said: "I kept back nothing that was profitable unto you, but have shewed you, and have taught you publicly, and from house to house, testifying both to the Jews, and also to the Greeks, repentance toward God, and faith toward our Lord Jesus Christ" (Acts 20: 20–21). Like Paul, Philip "ran" to proclaim the gospel, to discharge his responsibility, to share with those around him the deposit of faith and the immense amount of love and grace which filled his heart. Philip *ran* to do it.

On a number of occasions, I heard Gipsy Rodney Smith preach. What an experience it was, not only to watch him, but to be moved by his Spirit-filled and eloquent ministry! I saw many souls brought to the Lord through his earnest preaching; indeed, some in my own family circle came to Christ in his meetings. But there is one story I often think of in connection with Gipsy Smith. After the conclusion of a service, in which he had preached the gospel to many thousands, as the result of which scores had come to Christ, he left the building and hailed a taxi to take him home. But before he reached his destination, he had led the taxi-driver to Christ! You see, here was a man who, like Philip, *ran* about his Master's business, and up to the end of his wonderful life of service for the Lord, he never lost that note of urgency.

(4) *Philip ran because he saw a soul needing to be saved, and he longed to lead that soul to Christ.*

And he did lead him to Christ! And how eagerly, wisely, courageously and definitely he did this work of soul-saving! He was qualified because he knew the gospel; he knew how to explain the way of salvation; he knew his scriptures well; and he knew how to introduce the seeking sinner to the seeking Saviour. But, it took courage for Philip to run and do this job of work. I have tried to imagine myself in his place, only in a modern setting. Suppose I am walking along a London street and there is a hold-up in the flow of traffic. Suddenly I notice that in one of the cars our own Chancellor of the Exchequer is sitting and reading. What do I do? I immediately go up to the car, open the door, and say to him: "Excuse me, sir! What are you reading? Do you understand what you are reading?" (Of course, he might be reading the *Financial Times*!) You see what an audacious thing that would be for me to do? And yet this, in a way, is what Philip did. He saw men and women as souls for whom Christ had died and who needed to be saved through faith in Him. Do we long to lead men and women to the Saviour?

There are two ways of responding to a knock on the door. The first way is to say, "Oh, bother! Who's that calling at the door, and interrupting me!" But the other way is to say, "I wonder who that is knocking on the door? Perhaps it is someone to whom I can witness for the Lord!" There are two ways of having to follow a dusty chariot through the desert: the first way is to say, "Oh, this wretched dust! It's getting into my eyes, and ears and mouth! I must wait until the chariot in front has driven away!" But the other way is to say, "I wonder

14

who that is in the chariot? He looks very important. He needs to hear about the Saviour!" There are two ways of anticipating preaching engagements: the first way is to say, "Well – it's Sunday again, and I've got to preach two sermons!" That is unworthy; may God forgive any preacher who has fallen into such a backslidden state that he has lost the sense of his calling and the dignity and the sacredness of the Christian ministry! The second way is to say, "Hallelujah! It's Sunday again! What a marvellous opportunity I have of preaching the Word!" Nothing thrills me so much as preaching the unsearchable riches of Christ; besides which, the gospel is the only thing, the only message, that can meet the deepest need of men and women!

Philip could have said that "the love of Christ" constrained him and made him *run* to bring others to Jesus (2 Cor. 5: 14). He ran – and how worthwhile it was! He witnessed directly to only one soul, so far as the record tells us. When Philip ran up to the queen's treasurer, and climbed up into his chariot, the man must have been very startled. However, he was obviously a man with a deep spiritual hunger, for he did not repulse this stranger; on the other hand, he was delighted that here was someone who could help him. What a miracle it was that at that moment he was reading from Isaiah, chapter 53! This portion of scripture above all others explains our Lord's humiliation on the cross as He died to purchase our salvation. Philip did not focus the Ethiopian's attention upon religion, the Church, or Christians; he "preached unto him Jesus" (verse 35). Philip must also have instructed him in other basic truths concerning the Christian life, for as they came near an expanse of water, the new convert made a remarkable statement: "What," he asked, "doth hinder me to be baptised?" "And Philip said, If thou believest with all thine heart, thou mayest. And he answered and said, I believe that Jesus Christ is the Son of God . . . and he baptised him" (verses 36–38). Everyone in his entourage would have gathered round to watch this strange ordinance of Believers' Baptism, and we can be quite sure that Philip explained to them what he was doing and why he was doing it. What an amazing day this proved to be in the life of Queen Candace's treasurer! He then went on his way rejoicing; he had found the Saviour and had confessed him openly, all because Philip *ran* to him and led him to Christ.

(5) *Philip ran because he knew that every soul saved forges a link in the chain of the fulfilment of God's purposes.*

As we have noticed, the record tells us of the conversion of only one man – but what an important man he was! His conversion would have made startling headlines in the national newspapers: "Chancellor of Exchequer Converted on Way Home from Jerusalem!" But what an influence this man would have in his own country; and, in fact, in the purpose of God it was through this one man that the gospel went down into darkest Africa.

We certainly never know who we may be leading to Christ, when, in obedience to the Lord, we proclaim the gospel with urgency and with definiteness. That boy in our Sunday school class; that visitor to our Sunday service; that man with whom we talked in the bus; that passer-by to whom we spoke of Christ – who knows what God may do with any one of these when He has saved them and filled them with the Holy Spirit?

It is significant that the narrative in Acts 8 concludes with Philip still running – well, not exactly running, but being "caught away" and taken right out of the picture. For, "when they were come up out of the water, the Spirit of the Lord caught away Philip," and he was seen no more. Afterwards, however, he was found at Azotus (verses 39 and 40).

This is the kind of man whom God can use: a preacher in a hurry! Why was he in a hurry? Because when he heard God's commands he was eager to obey them; he realised that the gospel was a trust he must share with others; he knew this business for God was urgent; he had a passion to see guilty sinners saved; and he recognised that every soul saved is a link forged in the chain of God's purposes. And what was the secret of all this? We find this in Acts 6: 3 and 5, where we read that he was one of the seven Spirit-filled men chosen by the early Church "to serve tables". At the end of this fascinating story we find that Philip is lost sight of by the Ethiopian. A Spirit-filled man is always eager to get out of the picture and leave the glory and the results to God.

# 2 : Who is This?

*And they that sat at meat with Him began to
say within themselves, Who is this that forgiveth sins also?* (Luke 7: 49–50)

Simon was a Pharisee, a very strict religionist, and he
was so much more concerned with the outwardness of
his religion than with the inwardness of spirituality, that it
is surprising to learn that he invited Jesus to have a meal
at his house. We do not know what motive prompted him
to issue this invitation, whether it was concern, curiosity
or hostility, but we do know that the Lord Jesus welcomed
and accepted the invitation.

At this meal, there were a number of other people present, and as they sat together, talking and eating, an unin-
vited woman slipped in and stood behind Jesus. She was
evidently in very great distress; she was weeping bitterly,
and as her tears poured down her face and on to the feet
of Jesus, she stooped and wiped them away with her hair,
after which she kissed His feet. She then opened a small
alabaster box and she anointed His feet with the precious
and costly nard which it contained; immediately the
house was filled with a very lovely odour, so that everyone's attention was focussed upon Jesus and the dis-
tressed woman.

Simon the Pharisee was watching all this, and he was
filled with revulsion, and he reasoned in his heart, "This
man Jesus can't possibly know who this woman is! She is
a common harlot, a prostitute! Surely, if He knew that,
He wouldn't let her touch Him!" (verse 39). But Jesus
did know all about this woman; moreover, He knew all
about Simon. He knew exactly what this proud Pharisee
was thinking, and so He told a parable, and made an
application of the parable, which must have searched and
convicted Simon in his conscience. The Lord then turned
to the woman, and in the presence of all the watching
guests at the meal, He told her that all her sins were for-

given, and that through faith she had been saved and had received the pardon and the peace of God. What an amazing thing this was!

When those who were present heard Jesus say this, they began to ask, one after another: "Who is this . . .?"

I want to ask and to answer this question too: "Who is this . . .?" Who was in their midst that day? What can we say about Him? For He is the same today as yesterday (Heb. 13: 8). Who is this?

(1) *He is the One who knows all there is to know about us, and He loves us just the same.*

The Lord is omniscient; nothing is hidden from "the eyes of Him with whom we have to do" (Heb. 4: 13); "The eyes of the Lord are in every place, beholding the evil and the good" (Prov. 15: 3); and each one of us can say with Hagar of old: "Thou God seest me" (Gen. 16: 13). We cannot possibly hide anything from God. Everything is uncovered and open to Him.

Simon said to himself: "This man, if He were a prophet, would have known who and what manner of woman this is that toucheth Him: for she is a sinner" (verse 39). But Jesus did know that! He knew also everything about Simon as well, for: "Jesus answering said unto him, Simon, I have somewhat to say unto thee" (verse 40). And notice this very significant thing: in verse 39, we are told that Simon "spake within himself" – not audibly, but inwardly; and in verse 40, we are told that Jesus answered him . . .! You see, the Lord knew all that was going on in the heart and the mind of the Pharisee, as well as all that was going on in the heart and the mind of the sinful woman. How different they were! One was a self-righteous Pharisee; the other was a woman of the streets.

It would seem that these two people differed from each other in at least five ways. They were different *socially*: in all probability one lived on the outskirts of the city, in the residential area; the other lived in the haunts of the city where evil was rampant. They were different *morally*:

one was outwardly decent; the other was a prostitute. They were different *financially*: one was well set up in a material sense; the other was so poor that she sold her body to get a living. They were different *religiously*: one was very religious, a Pharisee; the other was probably quite irreligious. They were different *emotionally*: one was cold, calculating and hard; the other was warm, tender-hearted, and in the presence of many people she wept and kissed the feet of Jesus. These two people were totally different, and yet in one respect they were exactly the same; they were both sinners.

In verse 40, Jesus said to Simon: "I have somewhat to say unto thee . . ."; and He then told a parable, the point of which Simon could not fail to see. He said: "There was a certain creditor which had two debtors: the one owed five hundred pence, and the other fifty. And when they had nothing to pay, he frankly forgave them both"; and then Jesus said, and I am sure He was looking right into Simon's eyes as He said it: "Tell Me therefore, which of them will love him most?" The parable illustrated the fact that in God's sight both Simon and the woman were sinners, and therefore they were exactly the same. It is true that whereas Simon was a "fifty pence" sinner, the woman was a "five hundred pence" sinner; but in Romans 3: 22–23 we read: "There is no difference: for all have sinned, and come short of the glory of God"; and in James 2: 10, we are told that: "Whosoever shall keep the whole law, and yet offend in one point, he is guilty of all." In the sight of God, therefore, Simon was just as needy as the sinful woman.

It is exceedingly difficult to convince men and women that the respectable, religious, good-living man needs salvation just as much as the prostitute or the murderer. Certainly this woman was a sinner; her life had been ugly, sordid and horrible, and every such person needs the Saviour. Thank God, Jesus can save from the very worst sin! He can save those who are morally down-and-out; but, He can also save people, like Simon, who might be described as an "up-and-out". Maybe you come into that category. You are good, decent and honest, but you have never seen yourself as God sees you, and you have not yet realised that you are a needy sinner, and as such you are lost.

Jesus knew the very worst about these two people, but He loved them in spite of their sin, and He longed to deliver them from it and its consequences. Did He really love this sinful woman? Yes, He did! And He loves you – whoever you are, and whatever you have done. In eternity past, He knew how much you would need His salvation and His deliverance, and in God's time He left Heaven and came to this earth to die for you. Then He rose again, and now, through the agency of His Holy Spirit, He lives and waits to pardon you, to shed abroad His love in your heart and to make you the man or the woman He wants you to be. This is the gospel, the good news that "God commendeth His love toward us, in that, while we were yet sinners, Christ died for us" (Rom. 5: 8).

Who is this? He is the One who knows all about us, and loves us with an infinite love. But notice a second answer to this question.

(2) *He is the One who alone can forgive our sins and give us the assurance of salvation.*

In verses 47 and 48, we read that Jesus said to Simon: "I say unto thee, Her sins, which are many, are forgiven." He then turned to the woman and said: "Thy sins are forgiven!"; and it was at this point that those sitting at the meal with Him said, "Who is this that forgiveth sins also?" (verse 49).

Can you enter into the feelings of this sinful woman when she heard the Lord announce that her sins were forgiven? That is what she wanted above everything else, and she must have been overwhelmed with a sense of release and of gratitude. Yet, alas, there are thousands of people today who are bearing the weight of unforgiven sin. By His death upon the cross, our Lord has provided a full and a free salvation to all who will trust Him and

21

take it from Him in faith, but this wonderful offer is so often rejected. Have you been forgiven? Have you thanked the Lord Jesus for His salvation? God's Word makes it perfectly clear that you need to be forgiven; for you have not only sinned against yourself, against society, but you have sinned against God. You can do nothing to erase your past record of sin. The Bible says: "God requireth that which is past" (Eccles. 3:15), and reformation or turning over a new leaf cannot blot out your sins of the past. But there is wonderful news: the Lord Jesus will forgive you if you will come to Him and trust Him. Look carefully at these verses, and you will see that they declare emphatically the purpose for which Christ came into the world, and they assure us of His willingness to forgive, cleanse and save all who will trust Him.

"Come now, and let us reason together, saith the Lord: though your sins be as scarlet, they shall be as white as snow; though they be red like crimson, they shall be as wool" (Isa. 1:18).

"Thou shalt call His name Jesus: for He shall save His people from their sins" (Matt. 1: 21).

"This is a faithful saying, and worthy of all acceptation, that Christ Jesus came into the world to save sinners; of whom I am chief" (1 Tim. 1: 15).

These statements from God's Word make it abundantly clear that He can and He will forgive us, if we will accept His forgiveness; and He is the only One who can do it. Why is this?

Well, there are three reasons why only the Lord Himself can forgive us our sin. The first reason is that He is the offended party, the One against whom we have sinned. Therefore, if we are to receive forgiveness, we must receive it from Him. The second reason is that He has died to provide forgiveness. Of Him alone can we sing:

He died that we might be forgiven,
He died to make us good,
That we might go at last to Heaven,
Saved by his precious blood.

*Cecil Frances Alexander*

No one else has done this; He is the only Saviour: "Neither is there salvation in any other: for there is none other name under Heaven given among men, whereby we must be saved" (Acts 4: 12). He is the only One through whom a full and free pardon is offered: "Be it known unto you therefore, men and brethren, that through this man is preached unto you the forgiveness of sins: and by Him all that believe are justified from all things, from which ye could not be justified by the law of Moses" (Acts 13: 38–39). And the third reason why the Lord is the only One who can forgive us our sins is that He is alive now, and He is waiting to pardon us. This is the meaning of Hebrews 7: 25: "Wherefore He is able also to save them to the uttermost that come unto God by Him, seeing He ever liveth to make intercession for them."

But surely it is a presumption for anyone to say that he knows he is forgiven? Not at all! It was Jesus Himself who said, "Wherefore I say unto thee, Her sins, which are many, are forgiven"; it was Jesus Himself who turned to the woman and said, "Thy ... sins ... are ... forgiven!" I implore you not to rest until you know that your sins are forgiven.

Who is this? He is the One who knows all there is to know about us, and loves us just the same; He is the One who alone can forgive us our sins and give us the assurance of salvation; but there is one more truth revealed to us in this incident.

(3) *He is the One who saves us and gives us His peace the moment we believe in Him.*

Perhaps you are saying: "I want to be forgiven. I want to be saved. What must I do?" You must believe: "And

23

He said to the woman, Thy faith hath saved thee; go in peace" (verse 50). She was saved by faith alone, plus nothing; it was because she believed on the Lord Jesus Christ and received His forgiveness that she was saved. She had come to Him burdened with her sin; she had cast herself upon His mercy and had trusted Him to help her, cleanse her and forgive her. And what happened? He forgave her on the grounds of her faith. Faith takes what Jesus offers, and when you have taken what He offers, and only then, He will say to you: "Go in peace"; or, as it reads literally: "Go into peace" (verse 50). In other words, when our sins are forgiven, and when the Lord saves us, then we begin a new life of peace; we have "peace *with* God through our Lord Jesus Christ" (Rom. 5: 1); we have "the peace *of* God, which passeth all understanding" to keep our hearts and minds through Christ Jesus (Phil. 4: 7); and He gives us His power to go out and to live an entirely new life.

A very remarkable story is told concerning Lord Congleton. He spent some time in India, during the last century, serving the Lord as a missionary, but after a time he returned to England and settled on his estate. He was an ardent Christian, with a great passion for souls, and he was generous-hearted too. One day, copies of a notice appeared in various places round the village which was part of his estate. It read as follows:

Lord Congleton will be present with his steward at his office in the village between the hours of 9 and 12, on Tuesday, the 14th instant, and will there pay freely all accounts and debts to whomsoever due of any of his tenants who cannot discharge their obligations. To avail themselves of this offer, the applicants must present their accounts in the form of separate bills, containing an exact statement of the amount and nature of the debts owing to each creditor; and they must also give a statement of their own means and whatsoever property they have.

(signed) CONGLETON

This notice set the village talking! Crowds gathered round the various placards throughout the village and at the office. Some thought they would inquire at the steward's office to see what it meant; some thought Lord Congleton was crazy, but no one believed the notice they had read. On the appointed day, Lord Congleton and his steward arrived at the office by carriage; they dismounted and went into the office, shutting the door behind them. For almost two hours they sat there, and not one villager came to see them! Then, at eleven o'clock, an old couple, who were very poor, came to the office. "Is it true," they asked, "that Lord Congleton has offered to pay our debts?" "Yes." "Has anyone been in to see him?" "No, not yet," they were told. Then the old man looked at the notice on the door. "Why, wife," he exclaimed, "that's his lordship's signature! He'll keep his word! Thank God, we can die free from debt!" After a preliminary time of conversation, Lord Congleton said to the old couple, "Why should I pay your debts?" "I don't know," said the old man, "except that I saw your signature, and I believe your promise." "That is enough!" said Lord Congleton; and turning to his clerk, he said, "Draw out a cheque for the full amount." This was done, and the excited couple said, "We must go and tell our neighbours!" "Stop! Stop!" said Congleton. "They must trust my word, just as you did!" The couple were taken to another room, to wait for midday, and while he talked with them, Lord Congleton heard of their many misfortunes, as the result of which he gave them a cottage in which they could live for the rest of their days. When twelve o'clock came, Lord Congleton went to the office door and faced the crowd outside. He shook his head sadly, as he said, "My friends, I gave you the opportunity to come, and I would have paid your debts, but you would not believe me. I am sorry, but it is now past midday, and it is too late for you to take advantage of my offer." He and his steward went away in the carriage very sorrowfully. His generous offer had been made to every villager, but only two people had taken him at his word!

The Lord's offer of salvation is still open; but no one can say how long it will remain open. He is the One who knows all about you and loves you just the same; He is the One who alone can forgive you your sins and give you the assurance of salvation; and He is the One who saves you and gives you His peace the moment you believe in Him. Will you thank Him for His love? Will you receive His gracious offer of forgiveness for all your sins? Will you trust Him to save you now? Then your heart will be full of praise, and you will be able to say:

> Thank You, Lord, for saving my soul,
> Thank You, Lord, for making me whole,
> Thank You, Lord, for giving to me
> Thy great salvation, so rich and free.

# 3 : If this Book is True . . . ?

*Thy word is true from the beginning: and every one of Thy righteous judgments endureth for ever* (Ps. 119: 160)

What does the psalmist mean when he says: "Thy word is true from the beginning?" He means that God's word, like Himself, is true, and is therefore utterly reliable. It has been true from the first moment in which it was spoken, true throughout the whole of history, true for us from the moment we believed it, and it always will be true, for it "endureth for ever". David says a similar thing about God's testimonies in Psalm 119: 144, where he states that they are "everlasting", and in verse 152, he says: "I have known of old that Thou hast founded them for ever."

It is a great consolation to us to know that we also can say: "Thy word is true from the beginning: and every one of Thy righteous judgments endureth for ever." We may legitimately apply these words to the Bible, which God has graciously given to us and which is in very truth His Word. The Bible is true from the beginning. As Spurgeon says, when commenting on this verse: "The scriptures are as true in Genesis as in Revelation, and the five books of Moses are as inspired as the four Gospels . . . Against the decisions of the Lord no writ of error can be demanded, neither will there ever be a repealing of any of the acts of His sovereignty. There is not one single mistake either in the word of God or in the providential dealings of God. Neither in the book of revelation nor of providence will there be any need to put a single note of *errata*. The Lord has nothing to regret or to retract, nothing to amend or to reverse."

How grateful we should be that in this world of uncertainty there is a Book which speaks with absolute authority concerning the important things which we need to know! Yes, without any question, I join testimony with those who say: "Thy word is true from the beginning." I would not have given so many years of my life to preaching the gospel, declaring the truths of God, unfolding the revelation which God has given us in His Word, had I harboured any doubts at all about the absolute trustworthiness and authority of the Bible from Genesis to Revelation.

If we did not have a divine revelation, we would have no foundation for our faith, no rule to live by, no pillow to lay our heads on when we pass from time into eternity. We would be bewildered in the time of trouble and trial, and overwhelmed in the midst of sorrow and bereavement. We would be desolate indeed if we had no Bible in which we could find God's sure word to help us concerning the problems and perplexities of living, and the necessity of being prepared for dying. We would know nothing of the life to come; we would be left to man's speculations, and what good are they? Thank God that "all scripture is given by inspiration of God" (2 Tim. 3: 16).

Have you ever thought of the tremendous transformation which would take place in the world if the Bible were believed and accepted as the truth of God? If all our statesmen believed the Bible and acted upon the truth contained in it, there would be a great change in their government and in their handling of the affairs of our nation. They would look into this Book and up to the God of all wisdom, and He would help them, and there would be a very different world for us to live in. Imagine what would happen if men and women everywhere accepted the testimony of the psalmist and believed that God's Word is true through and through! God's laws would be obeyed and His Name would be honoured, and the fearful things which are taking place in the world would be on the decrease, instead of on the increase; the crime wave would be halted; standards of truth and righteousness would prevail; and solutions would be found for the gigantic and devilish problems which are facing our human race. What a tragedy it is that men, to whom God in His love has given His Word, have rejected it!

I heard a lovely story which concerned an elderly couple. They were decent people and were loved and respected by their family and their neighbours – but they were not Christians. As a matter of fact, they were not even church-goers, and although they were getting on in years they knew very little about the things of God. Someone, however, became interested in them and persuaded them to attend an evangelistic service in a church near their home. Everything they heard that night was new to them, and when they arrived back home, the husband said to his wife, "You know, I believe we're wrong. We ought not to have neglected reading the Bible all these years. Let's read it together every night, shall we?" So they began to read the Bible regularly. A few nights later, as he finished reading, the husband closed the book and said, "I've come to a conclusion, and that is – if this Book is true, *we are sinners*." His wife nodded her head. "Yes," she said, "I believe you are right." They continued with their reading, and a day or two later, the husband stopped at the end of a verse, and said, "I say, dear, if this Book is true, you and I are not only sinners – but *we are lost!*" His wife answered, "Yes, I feel exactly as you do. The Bible certainly says that we're lost!" and they retired to bed feeling very unhappy. However, this did not stop them reading the Book, and a night or two later he said, "Do you realise that if this Book is true, *we can be saved*, if we will accept Jesus Christ as our Saviour?" "Oh, I'm so glad to hear you say that!" exclaimed his wife, "for I believe it too!" and they knelt down together and asked the Lord Jesus Christ to come into their lives and to be their Saviour. At the conclusion of their next night's reading, the husband turned to his wife, with a beaming face, and he said, "Isn't it wonderful! If this Book is true, *we are saved!*" She smiled too, as she said, "Yes, if this Book is true, we are!" This is a true incident, but it wonderfully illustrates the way in which anyone, anywhere, can come into the full assurance of salvation. Consider the four discoveries made by this elderly couple who became Christians so late in life.

(1) *If this Book is true, we are sinners.*

This was a great discovery for these two people to make. They had tried to live decent lives, but now they had made a tremendous discovery. They were sinners! Think of it! They had lived all those years before the fact actually sank into their understanding that in God's sight they were sinners, and therefore they needed a Saviour.

I remember a lady who started to come to our services. After she had been attending regularly for some weeks, she came to me and said, "When I came to the first few services here, I thought that because I had always done my best, then that was all right. I have honestly tried to live a good life, but tonight, while you were preaching, I realised, as I have never realised before, how sinful I am in the sight of a holy God!"

Well, she was right. If this Book is true, you and I are sinners, because this Book says we are sinners. The Bible says: "There is none righteous, no, not one . . . for all have sinned, and come short of the glory of God" (Rom. 3: 10 and 23). The king in his palace, the beggar in the slum, the rich and the poor, the young and the old, the literate and the illiterate – "There is not a just man upon earth, that doeth good, and sinneth not" (Eccles. 7: 20). This Book tells us that we were born in sin: "Wherefore, as by one man sin entered into the world, and death by sin; and so death passed upon all men, for that all have sinned . . ." (Rom. 5: 12). The psalmist actually confessed: "Behold, I was shapen in iniquity; and in sin did my mother conceive me" (Ps. 51: 5); and the prophet Jeremiah reminds us that: "The heart is deceitful above all things, and desperately wicked: who can know it?" (Jer. 17: 9.) Do you know your own heart? In God's sight it is vile and wretched. We all need to say with Peter: "Depart from me; for I am a sinful man, O Lord" (Luke

5: 8); and with the Prodigal: "I have sinned against Heaven, and in Thy sight, and am no more worthy to be called Thy son" (Luke 15: 21). If this Book is true, we are sinners.

## (2) *If this Book is true, we are lost.*

We are not only sinners, but we are in a helpless, hopeless and lost condition, because our sin has separated us from God (Isa. 59: 1–2). God is holy, and "all we like sheep have gone astray; we have turned every one to his own way" (Isa. 53: 6). This is the very essence of sin. Sin is turning from God's way to our way; it is rebellion against God. Therefore, because the universal verdict is that we have all turned to our own way, we are therefore all sinners – lost sinners, because God and sin cannot live together. This is the meaning of the words: "The wages of sin is death" (Rom. 6: 23); and death means separation from God, in a spiritual sense. Sin puts a barrier between the soul and God, and this is what it means to be lost. It means to be out of fellowship with Him, out of harmony with Him and unable to come into His holy presence . . . lost!

On one occasion, a little boy was found wandering along the road. A constable stopped him, and as he could not understand what the little fellow was trying to say, he took him back to the police station and sat him down. The little boy was so tired that he fell asleep immediately. "Hallo! What's that youngster doing here?" asked another constable. "Sh!" warned the first constable. "Don't wake him up! He's lost – but he doesn't know it yet!" I wonder whether you have ever come to the point where you have realised your lost condition. If you do not know Jesus Christ as your Saviour, then I want to tell you on the authority of God's Word, which is true from the beginning, that you are lost at this moment. What a dangerous condition to be in! You are lost to Heaven, lost to Jesus, lost to all that is noblest and best; you are lost now, and if something is not done about it, you will be lost for ever!

I shall never forget a man whom I went to counsel after a preaching service. He was obviously in deep distress, and I asked him if I could be of any help to him. "Yes, you can!" he said. "I have realised for the first time that I'm lost!" You know, it is a great thing when a man comes to that point. It is a great thing to accept the testimony of God's Word concerning our spiritual condition. Jesus once told a parable about a lost sheep. There were one hundred sheep in the flock, but when they were counted it was found that ninety-nine were safely in the fold – but one was missing (Luke 15: 4). What a discovery to make! not only that you are a sinner, but that you are a lost sinner! Can anything be done about it? Yes, thank God!

(3) *If this Book is true, we can be saved.*

This is the gospel of the grace of God; it is the good news of God's love for us all; that lost people can be found. There are hundreds of statements in the Bible which prove that lost sinners can be saved. Let me give you some of them from the Book, and notice that all of them make it clear that "whosoever will" may be saved.

*Isaiah 45: 22:* Look unto Me, and be ye saved, all the ends of the earth: for I am God, and there is none else.

*Matthew 9: 13:* I am not come to call the righteous, but sinners to repentance.

*Luke 19: 10:* The Son of man is come to seek and to save that which was lost.

*John 3:16* For God so loved the world, that He gave His only begotten Son, that whosoever believeth in Him should not perish, but have everlasting life.

*John 5: 24:* Verily, verily, I say unto you, He that heareth My word, and believeth on Him that sent Me, hath everlasting life, and shall not come into condemnation; but is passed from death unto life.

*John 10: 9:* I am the door: by Me if any man enter in, he shall be saved, and shall go in and out, and find pasture.

*Romans 1: 16:* I am not ashamed of the gospel of Christ: for it is the power of God unto salvation to every one that believeth; to the Jew first, and also to the Greek.

*2 Peter 3: 9:* The Lord is not slack concerning His promise, as some men count slackness; but is longsuffering to us-ward, not willing that any should perish, but that all should come to repentance.

*Revelation 22: 17:* And the Spirit and the bride say, Come. And let him that heareth say, Come. And let him that is athirst come. And whosoever will, let him take the water of life freely.

These verses mean that anybody, anywhere, at any time and in any condition, can be saved: they mean that any man who sees that he is a lost sinner can be saved by Jesus Christ the moment he puts his faith in Him. Do you wonder that I have rejoiced in preaching this gospel down the years? It is wonderful to be able to tell people about the love of God in Christ, and to invite them to put their trust in the Saviour, so that they may live for Him day by day and dwell with Him through all eternity. What good news it is that anyone can trust Christ now and know that he is not a lost sinner but a saved sinner! If you do not know this, you may have this glad assurance at this moment.

One of the things I like about the story of the elderly couple who came to know the Lord is that they made a fourth discovery. Many people accept the Lord as their Saviour, but they lack the absolute assurance that they are saved, and they doubt whether the Lord really has accepted them. This need not be so, and it is certainly not glorifying to God. So, I am glad to tell you that the story of the husband and his wife concludes with their fourth discovery.

(4) *If this Book is true, we are saved.*

If you will turn back to the scriptures quoted above, you will discover that all the way through them the note of assurance is sounded out. God invites us to trust Him; He tells us that when we put our trust in Him, He saves us, cleanses us, forgives us, makes us His own, and makes us secure. This means that the moment anyone turns to Him in faith, and puts his whole trust in Him as his Saviour and Lord, he may then at once say: "If this Book is true, then I *am* saved! I don't deserve it, I haven't earned it – but if this Book is true, my sins are forgiven, the Lord Jesus is living in my heart, I am on my way to Heaven, and in the meantime He will give me power to live for Him day by day!"

It is not a presumption to say we are sure we are saved; it is simply a matter of taking God at His word, of believing what He says and of rejoicing that He has kept His word and fulfilled His promise. It is a greater presumption to doubt what He says.

Of course this Book is true; it is absolutely true! "Thy word is true from the beginning." Thank God it is so!

# 4 : God's Happy People

*Blessed is the man that trusteth in Him . . . and
none of them that trust in Him shall be desolate* (Ps. 34: 8 and 22)

I want to show you from God's Word that it is His plan
and purpose for every one of His children to be really
happy. We have to confess, however, that very often we
are unhappy people. Even our conscious fellowship with
our Lord Jesus is too frequently overshadowed by our
own troubles and self-centredness, and we endure our
prayer time rather than rejoice in it.

In this thirty-fourth Psalm, there are two phrases
which I want to join together. In verse 8, David says:
"Blessed is the man that trusteth in Him": and in verse 22
he says: "And none of them that trust in Him shall be
desolate." Now, before we look further into these words,
it would be well for us to realise that the word "blessed",
in simple terms, means "happy", and the word "desolate" means "unhappy". What David is saying then is
this: "Happy is the man that trusteth in Him . . . and
none of them that trust in Him shall be unhappy!" Now,
what are the grounds of our happiness? Psalm 34 supplies the answer.

(1) *God's people are happy because they have all their
thoughts established.*

In verse 1, we read: "I will bless the Lord at all times:
His praise shall continually be in my mouth." These are
the words of a truly happy man. But what are the most
important words in this verse? I believe they are the
words "all" and "continually". David is saying,
"Whether things are pleasing or painful, whether the sun
is shining or the sky is clouded, I will bless the Lord at *all*
times! He is my loving heavenly Father, and all my times
are in His hand. He is planning my pathway, and if I am
in the midst of trouble or distress, it is quite all right. He

has not altered in any way. My thoughts about God and my Father are established; they do not waver, so that one day I think He loves me, and then the next day I question His loving wisdom!"

If you have read the biography of C. T. Studd, you will remember that the time came when this soul-burdened missionary statesman was to return to Central Africa for what proved to be the last time. Mrs Studd realised that she would probably never see her beloved husband again on earth, and anyway this was going to mean years of separation for the two of them. She picked up her *Daily Light*, and she read: "I will bless the Lord at *all* times: His praise shall *continually* be in my mouth!" Humanly speaking, it was impossible for her to be happy in such circumstances, but because her thoughts were established in her God, she rejoiced!

This is what I mean by having our thoughts established. Some Christians are only happy when everything pleases them, and when they can trace, or think they can trace, God's dealings with them. But others, like the psalmist, know that because He is their gracious and loving Father who is planning their lives for them, then all things are working together for their good and for His glory (Rom. 8: 28); so they praise the Lord and bless His holy Name at all times. That is the first ground of the Christian's happiness. God's people are happy because they have all their thoughts established.

> Through all the changing scenes of life,
>     In trouble and in joy,
> The praises of my God shall still
>     My heart and tongue employ.
>             *N. Tate and N. Brady*

When Paul and Silas, who were so wonderfully used of God in the days of the early Church, found themselves in prison, with bleeding backs and with their feet in the stocks, they began singing praises to God, even though it was midnight, because their thoughts of Him and of His dealings with them were established. Their joy was not affected by their circumstances, for the "Spirit of glory and of God" rested upon them in their time of testing (1 Pet. 4: 14).

(2) *God's people are happy because they have all their fears banished.*

In verse 4, we read: "I sought the Lord, and He heard me, and delivered me from all my fears." What is the most important word in this verse? Well, surely it is that same word "all"! That covers every kind of fear; and how wonderful it is to have all our fears banished! Someone once said to me, "If I could get rid of all my fears, I'd be the happiest person in the world!" I replied, "Well, you can! The Lord can free you from your fears; and I know what I am saying, because I have proved it."

What is your fear? It may be the fear of living. Doctors tell us that there is an anxiety neurosis gripping the hearts and minds of multitudes of people throughout the world. It is fear of the unknown future, fear of failure, fear of old age, fear of illness, fear of the repetition of some trial or dark experience, or fear concerning a loved one. Are you gripped by a fear? Then I want to tell you that the Lord Jesus is able and wanting to banish your fear. What did the psalmist do when he was gripped by fear? He says: "I sought the Lord, and He heard me, and delivered me from all my fears!" (verse 4). "Oh!" you say, "how I should like to have my fears banished!" You can! And if your fears are banished, then the Lord will release into your life a joy and a peace which you have never known, nor ever could know, while you have been bound by fear, and you will become the radiant, joyful Christian that God wants you to be.

God's people are happy because they have all their fears banished. Even as you read these words, the risen Lord is with you to banish your fear. He can deal with it, and He will say to you: "It is I; be not afraid" (Matt. 14: 27).

(3) *God's people are happy because they have all their sins covered.*

In verse 5 we read: "They looked unto Him, and were lightened: and their faces were not ashamed." It is impossible for us to look into the face of a holy God if our sin has not been covered, for we could not bear to look into the brightness of His holiness. With Isaiah, we would have to say, "Woe is me! . . . for mine eyes have seen the King . . ." (Isa. 6: 5). But in verse 5 of our psalm, we discover that here were some people who could look into the face of God: "They looked unto Him, and were lightened: and their faces were not ashamed." How can we look into the face of a holy God without being condemned and pronounced guilty? This is only possible because the Lord Jesus has died and has blotted out our sins.

In Psalm 32, David, who had sinned so greatly and so grievously, tells us about this. He says: "Blessed (happy) is he whose transgression is forgiven, whose sin is covered. Blessed (happy) is the man unto whom the Lord imputeth not iniquity, and in whose spirit there is no guile" (verses 1–2). Do you know the joy of sins forgiven? Do you know the happiness which comes when you boldly enter the presence of God, conscious of the fact that your sins have been covered by the blood-shedding of the Lord Jesus Christ, who has made atonement for your sins?

God's people are happy because they have all their sins covered, for "there is therefore now no condemnation to them which are in Christ Jesus" (Rom. 8: 1). That which covers them is the perfect, spotless, seamless robe of the righteousness of their Lord; their sin is covered, and that is the ground of their happiness. If you are a child of God, does this not make you rejoice "with joy unspeakable and full of glory" (1 Pet. 1: 8), when you realise that you can enter with boldness into the holiest of all (Heb. 10: 19)?

38

(4) *God's people are happy because they have all their prayers answered.*

In verses 6, 15 and 17, we read that: "This poor man cried, and the Lord heard him, and saved him out of all his troubles ... The eyes of the Lord are upon the righteous, and His ears are open unto their cry ... The righteous cry, and the Lord heareth, and delivereth them out of all their troubles."

Now here was a man who was in great trouble, and I am glad we are not told what his trouble was, for we might say, "But that's not my trouble; mine is quite different!" So, as we are not told what his trouble was, we can put our troubles right in here: "This poor man cried, and the Lord heard him, and saved him out of all his troubles." And what is the most important word here? It is that same little word "all", which occurs twice in these verses.

When the psalmist was in the midst of his troubles, what did he do? He prayed. Wise man! It is amazing how many Christians, who face testings and trials, try to deal with them in their own strength, while all the time God is waiting for them to pray, in order that He can help them.

A lady once said to me, "I'm in such trouble. Can I come and tell you all about it?" "Yes," I said, "we'll make an appointment. Will it need to be a long one?" "Well, yes," she said, "you see, I shall have to tell you the whole story. I'm in great trouble!" "Have you prayed about it?" I asked her. "Not really," she said. "Well," I said, "I'm going to suggest that you pray about it. Then, if you still want to come and talk about it, we'll make an appointment to meet." A day or two later she telephoned me, and her voice sounded very much happier. "Mr Dixon," she said, "I needn't take up your time. God has answered my prayer, and everything is going to be all right!" With all the promises which God has given us in His Word, and with all the encouragements which He gives us, as Christians, to come to Him with our needs, it is strange that we grope around, try this and that, go from this friend to that friend – when all we need to do is to commit the whole thing definitely into the hands of the Lord Himself and wait for Him to provide the solution or the enabling.

> Oh, what peace we often forfeit!
> Oh, what needless pain we bear!
> All because we do not carry
> Everything to God in prayer.
>
> *J. M. Scriven*

Have you a burden? If you will hand it to the Lord, He will undertake for you, for He says: "Call upon Me in the day of trouble: I will deliver thee, and thou shalt glorify Me" (Ps. 50: 15). This is the promise of a personal and a specific answer: "*I* will deliver *thee,* and *thou* shalt glorify *Me.*'

(5) *God's people are happy because they have all their enemies scattered.*

In verse 7, David tells us this: "The angel of the Lord encampeth round about them that fear Him, and delivereth them." If we belong to the Lord, we are in constant need of deliverance, for there are many foes at hand and around us; but we are absolutely safe. Why? Because we are protected by God's angels. We miss very much joy when we fail to count upon the ministry of the angels. In the Bible there is a whole body of revealed truth on the ministry of angels. For example:

Because thou hast made the Lord, which is my refuge, even the most High, thy habitation; there shall no evil befall thee, neither shall any plague come nigh thy dwelling. For He shall give His angels charge over thee, to keep thee in all thy ways. They shall bear thee up in their hands, lest thou dash thy foot against a stone (Ps. 91: 9–12).

Then said Daniel unto the king, O king, live for ever.

40

My God hath sent His angel, and hath shut the lions' mouths, that they have not hurt me (Dan. 6: 21–22).

Take heed that ye despise not one of these little ones; for I say unto you, That in Heaven their angels do always behold the face of My Father which is in Heaven (Matt. 18: 10).

Peter was sleeping between two soldiers, bound with two chains: and the keepers before the door kept the prison. And, behold, the angel of the Lord came upon him, and a light shined in the prison: and he smote Peter on the side, and raised him up, saying, Arise up quickly! . . . (Acts 12: 6–7).

Are they not all ministering spirits, sent forth to minister for them who shall be heirs of salvation? (Heb. 1: 14).

> The hosts of God encamp around
> The dwellings of the just;
> Deliverance He affords to all
> Who on His succour trust.
> *N. Tate and N. Brady*

God commissions His angels to come and watch over us. If you are going into hospital next week, remember that God's angels are going to be there too; if you are fearful about taking that journey, then remember that these unseen servants of the most High God will also be with you. That is why God's people are happy; they have the angels with them to protect them, and to scatter all their enemies.

(6) *God's people are happy because they have all their needs supplied.*

There are some wonderful words in verses 9 and 10: "O fear the Lord, ye His saints: for there is no want to them that fear Him. The young lions do lack, and suffer hunger: but they that seek the Lord shall not want any

41

good thing"; in other words, they will not lack anything which the Lord sees to be good for them. "The Lord is my shepherd: I shall not want" (Ps. 23: 1). John McNeill liked to quote Wordsworth in connection with this verse:

> The swan on still St Mary's lake
> Floats double, swan and shadow!

Wherever the swan goes, there goes the shadow. If the shadow is moving along St Mary's lake, then the swan must be there! And if the Lord is my shepherd, then I shall not want. How can I, if He is my shepherd? We cannot divorce the one from the other. "My God shall supply all your need according to His riches in glory by Christ Jesus" (Phil. 4: 19). "And He (Jesus) said unto them, When I sent you without purse, and scrip, and shoes, lacked ye any thing? And they said, Nothing!" (Luke 22: 35).

In Luke 12, we find a contrasting picture. First, there is that of the rich farmer who spoke proudly about "my barns!" He had many barns, but he had no God. Further down in this passage we read: "Consider the ravens: for they neither sow nor reap; which neither have storehouse nor barn ..." They have no barns at all, but "God feedeth them: how much more are ye better than the fowls?" (Luke 12: 16–21 and 24). Which is true of you? Have you barns, and no God?; or, have you God, and perhaps no barns? If we have God, then we shall lack nothing!

(7) *God's people are happy because their future is assured.*

We are told this in verses 21 and 22 of this thirty-fourth Psalm: "Evil shall slay the wicked: and they that hate the righteous shall be desolate. The Lord redeemeth the soul of His servants: and none of them that trust in Him shall be desolate (unhappy)." Here, the righteous and the unrighteous are set in contrast. The future of the one is blessed indeed; but the future of the other is almost too terrible to contemplate.

The future of the righteous is blessed; so whether we are upon the earth when the Lord comes back, or whether we shall have to pass through the veil of death before we see Him in the Glory, it does not matter, because our future is assured.

All our thoughts established; all our fears banished; all our sins covered; all our prayers answered; all our enemies scattered; all our needs supplied; and all our future assured! These things, and many others, are the sure ground of our happiness as believers in our God and in His Son Jesus Christ. Oh, how happy we should be! But let me emphasise this: we should be happy most of all because of Him in whom we find and experience all these wonderful blessings.

Fanny Crosby went blind when she was five, and she lived to be ninety-five. At the age of eight, she wrote these words:

> Oh, what a happy soul am I!
>     Although I cannot see,
> I am resolved that in this world
>     Contented I shall be.
> How many blessings I enjoy
>     That other people don't!
> To weep and sigh, because I'm blind,
>     I cannot, and I won't!

# 5 : A Row of Medicine Bottles

*What aileth thee?* (2 Sam. 14: 5)

Life is made up of excitements, to a greater or a lesser degree, and one small excitement I still experience each morning is finding out what the postman has brought me. Some letters bring great encouragement, others bring opportunities for giving help to those in need, and still others bring seed-thoughts for me to pick up and use if I wish. One morning I received a letter from a friend who suggested that I should preach on "A Row of Medicine Bottles", from Psalm 37; and from that seed-thought a sermon emerged, which I want now to pass on to you.

When I first read my friend's letter, I was curious to know what he meant; however, after thinking it over I began to see that there are times in the experience of each one of us when we feel unwell, and we know that we are in need of a dose of some kind of medicine. My dictionary tells me that medicine is "any substance used (especially internally) for the treatment or prevention of disease." Disease is really dis-ease, uneasiness or any want of health. We, as Christians, know that we are often dis-eased, or unwell, in a spiritual sense. It may be that that is our condition now; perhaps in a spiritual sense we are thoroughly out of sorts and we need some medicine.

Did you ever think of the Bible as a medicine cupboard? It is just that; and as I thought over the suggestion that I should preach on "A Row of Medicine Bottles", I opened the cupboard and examined some of the bottles on the shelf called Psalm 37. In the back of my mind was the question which King David asked of the woman of Tekoah long ago: "What aileth thee?" (2 Sam. 14: 5). What ails you? Are you in need of spiritual medicine? Then look with me into Psalm 37 and see how very

44

wonderfully God supplies the remedy for all our ills from the contents of the bottles on this shelf.

(1) *If you are troubled and perplexed about the prosperity of the wicked, take a good dose of verses 1 and 2.*

"Fret not thyself because of evildoers, neither be thou envious against the workers of iniquity. For they shall soon be cut down like the grass, and wither as the green herb." So said David, the psalmist. He was very perplexed, as many of God's people are, to see the wicked flourishing, prospering, and "getting away with it!" This state of affairs causes uneasiness; and if we are frank about it, as we look out into the world today it does seem to us that bad men, who have no love for God, and who deny Him and blaspheme His Name, seem to prosper. Every time we open our newspapers we read of evil forces of men and nations which are advancing victoriously, and all this is very upsetting and unsettling and perplexing. Murderers, robbers and revolutionaries perpetrate their devilish deeds, and then they seem to emerge scot-free. This was the problem of the psalmist; and it is to this very kind of situation that he refers in this psalm. What can be done about it? I will tell you. Take a dose of medicine from this psalm, for this was David's perplexity. What did he say about this? Verses 1 and 2 give us the answer: and if this bottle on the shelf does not do the trick, I suggest you need also to take a dose of verses 10, 13, 35 and 36: "For yet a little while, and the wicked shall not be: yea, thou shalt diligently consider his place, and it shall not be ... The Lord shall laugh at him: for He seeth that his day is coming ... I have seen the wicked in great power, and spreading himself like a green bay tree. Yet he passed away, and, lo, he was not: yea, I sought him, but he could not be found."

Take a good long draught from all these bottles, and as you do this you will be brought from your state of disease into a settled condition of heart and mind. You will recognise that God is sovereign in the affairs of men and nations, and that in His own good time He will step in and take control. You will also be filled with compassion for all those who do not know the Lord, as you realise that their time is short, and that soon God's judgment will fall upon them.

(2) *If your income seems to be dwindling and you are wondering how you are going to make ends meet, take a dose of verse 3.*

"Trust in the Lord, and do good; so shalt thou dwell in the land, and verily thou shalt be fed." The problem of supply is a very serious one, and it causes dis-ease with many people. The cost of living is rising so rapidly, and where is the provision coming from?

Elijah lived through a terrible drought, and he must have experienced times of doubt; but what did God say to him? "Hide thyself by the brook Cherith ... and it shall be, that thou shalt drink of the brook; and I have commanded the ravens to feed thee there. So he went and did according unto the word of the Lord ... and the ravens brought him bread and flesh in the morning, and bread and flesh in the evening; and he drank of the brook." Then, to Elijah's consternation, this source of supply dried up. Did he worry? He need not have done so, for God spoke again to him, and said, "Get thee to Zarephath ... I have commanded a widow woman there to sustain thee ..." (1 Kgs. 17: 3–16).

But there is another bottle on this shelf, and it contains verse 19: "They shall not be ashamed in the evil time: and in the days of famine they shall be satisfied"; and yet another bottle – verse 25: "I have been young, and now am old; yet have I not seen the righteous forsaken, nor his seed begging bread."

Do you remember the words which the Lord gave to Abraham when he was in desperate need? It was just this: "God will provide ..." (Gen. 22: 8). His name is El-Shaddai, which means He is "the enough God" (Gen. 17: 1). So, if you are troubled about the matter of provision, I suggest you take a really good dose of verse 3, and speed up the action by taking further doses from

verses 19 and 25. You can be quite sure of this: the Lord
has promised to look after you, and to provide for your
need, and He will, for "hath He said, and shall He not do
it?" (Num. 23: 19).

(3) *If you are depressed, downcast and impatient, and you
feel that God does not care, and even your prayers go
unanswered, take a dose of verses 4, 5, 6 and 7, both night
and morning.*

This is a strong dose, but how efficacious it is! "Delight
thyself also in the Lord; and He shall give thee the desires
of thine heart. Commit thy way unto the Lord: trust also
in Him; and He shall bring it to pass. And He shall bring
forth thy righteousness as the light, and thy judgment
as the noonday. Rest in the Lord, and wait patiently
for Him: fret not thyself . . ." It is so easy, when things
go wrong, to fall into a depressed and downcast condition and to feel that God no longer loves or cares for
us!

There is a story told of a man who had a pain in his leg,
so he consulted his doctor. After the doctor had examined the leg he gave his patient some pink pills, which he
assured him would soon put the leg right. The man then
said that he also had a pain in his shoulder, and after
further examination the doctor prescribed some green
pills for him. The man had one more thing to say.
"Doctor, how do the pink pills know how to go to my leg,
and how do the green pills know how to go to my shoulder?" You may well say to me, "How can these verses
banish my depression and my dread of the future and restore my confidence in God?" All I can say is this: take
the dose and try it for yourself. It works, for I have
proved it. But if you feel you need further encouragement
and some stronger medicament to liven you up, get alone
with Psalm 42 and enter into the experience of the psalmist; talk to yourself, and question yourself, as he did:
"Why art thou cast down, O my soul? and why art thou
disquieted within me?" But he did not stop there; he
continued, "Hope thou in God!" (Ps. 42: 11). So, rise

47

up in faith, and put your whole trust in the One who will never fail you.

(4) *If you are upset, angry, and you feel resentful and vindictive, take a regular dose of verse 8, especially if you feel an attack is coming on.*

This is what verse 8 says: "Cease from anger, and forsake wrath: fret not thyself in any wise to do evil."

It is the unexpected things which cause anger and resentment to rise up within us. Someone speaks an unkind word, or perhaps the unkind word is followed by a thoughtless action, and then anger rises up within us. The apostle Paul very wisely said to the Ephesian Christians: "Be ye angry, and sin not: let not the sun go down upon your wrath: neither give place to the Devil" (Eph. 4: 26–27). Barnes, the commentator, makes these verses read: "If you be angry, which may be the case, and which may be unavoidable, see that the sudden excitement does not become sin. Do not let it over-leap its proper bounds; do not cherish it; do not let it remain in your bosom, even to the setting of the sun. Though the sun be sinking in the west, let not the passion linger in the bosom, but let his last rays find you always peaceful and calm." What a word that is from the past! But even though it comes from a byegone age, it is absolutely up-to-date and applicable to us today. If we are not to let the sun go down upon our wrath, it means that we must take a dose of medicine before we go to bed; or, in other words, we are to get every wrong emotion out of our system, such as anger, bitterness, jealousy and resentment. We are to be at peace with God, with all men, and with ourselves before the day closes; and if only we would do this, how many problems and difficult situations would be quickly solved!

(5) *If you are filled with morbid fears and doubts about your salvation and your eternal security, take strong doses of verses 18, 24, 28 and 33.*

This is the prescription to banish doubt! "The Lord

knoweth the days of the upright: and their inheritance shall be for ever ... Though he fall, he shall not be utterly cast down: for the Lord upholdeth him with His hand ... For the Lord loveth judgment, and forsaketh not His saints; they are preserved for ever: but the seed of the wicked shall be cut off ... The Lord will not leave him in his hand, nor condemn him when he is judged.''

Many Christians lack the assurance of their salvation; they are filled with doubts as to whether God has accepted them, whether they are really saved or not, and whether the Lord will let them go out of His presence into outer darkness. How subtle the Devil is! Is this your dis-ease, your malady, and does it threaten you, especially in the night? Well, here is the remedy. Notice in the verses under this heading that the two words "for ever" occur twice, and that the Lord promises that even if we fail and fall we shall not fall out of His loving care, for He will uphold us with His own hand. If you lack assurance, there is only one way to gain it, or regain it: assurance comes by seeing what God says in His Word, and by taking Him at His word. Take the Word of God – and believe it! God says you are His, if you have put your trust in Him as your Saviour: therefore, you are safe and absolutely secure, for He will never let you go. Take a large dose of that!

(6) *If you are troubled about God's plan for your life, about God's guidance, about His interest in your job, your career or your future service, take a dose of verses 23 and 24.*

What a tremendous statement is contained in these two verses: "The steps of a good man are ordered by the Lord: and He delighteth in his way. Though he fall, he shall not be utterly cast down: for the Lord upholdeth him with His hand." We must always remember one thing when we are thinking about God's guidance, and it is this: the Lord is far more concerned to guide us along the pathway of His will than we are to be guided by Him; but if we will trust Him, lean upon Him, wait for Him and seek to please Him, He will unfailingly and un-falteringly guide us into ways which are pleasing to Him and profitable to us. Even if we stumble and fall, as indeed we do, and shall do, He will uphold us and lead us on. If you are a young man and you are concerned as to your future, let me urge you to take a dose of these verses; if you are a girl, and you long to marry the man of God's choice, then you should take this particular dose as well. It will settle you, establish you and take away all your dis-ease.

(7) *If you are in great trouble, you are tossed about and are at your wit's end, then take a dose of verse 39.*

"The salvation of the righteous is of the Lord: He is their strength in the time of trouble." Yes, He is our strength in the time of trouble; and this means that if you are in trouble at this moment, the Lord will see you through, if you will commit your case to Him. Take a dose of that, and see if you do not feel better already! The Lord will never fail you or forsake you; the Lord will never let you down or let you go. Take a good strong dose of that, and calm down!

Before I close the door of this wonderful medicine cupboard, I would like to say two things. The first is this: I have noticed that many medicine chests have a mirror on the front of them. God's medicine chest also has a mirror on it. As we come to it, we see ourselves, our true condition, reflected in this mirror, which is placed just at the right height and the right angle for us to see ourselves reflected in the glass. The second thing is this: when we open the door of this cupboard and see the rows of bottles, which contain the remedy for all our ills and sick-nesses, it is not enough for us just to look at them, or even to remove a cork or stopper and smell the contents. We must take a dose; we must take it internally.

Thus, in James 1: 21–25, we are exhorted: "Receive with meekness the engrafted word, which is able to save your souls. But be ye doers of the word, and not hearers only, deceiving your own selves. For if any be a hearer of the word, and not a doer, he is like unto a man beholding his natural face in a glass: for he beholdeth himself, and goeth his way, and straightway forgetteth what manner of man he was. But whoso looketh into the perfect law of liberty, and continueth therein, he being not a forgetful hearer, but a doer of the work, this man shall be blessed in his deed."

Are you well? How well are you? In his third epistle, the apostle John, writing to "the wellbeloved Gaius", says these amazing words: "I wish above all things that thou mayest prosper and be in health, even as thy soul prospereth" (3 John 2). If we were suddenly to become in our physical frames what we actually are in our spiritual lives, would we find ourselves as robust as Gaius was, or would we be as invalids and in sickly health? Are you sick? Are you ailing in your spiritual life? Well, "what aileth thee?" Take a look along this row of medicine bottles, and help yourself to a large dose of the appropriate cure. In this way you will be, as James says, blessed in your deed.

On one occasion, I was very unwell indeed, due to overwork, so I went to my doctor for a tonic. "I want something that will put me right by the end of the week," I said. "Well," he replied, "it may not work as quickly as that. I'll give you something that will put you right, but you must take it regularly and for some time. You see, you have been getting run down over a long period, and it will take time for you to pull up again. Take yourself in hand, and give yourself some weeks to regain your strength. This medicine will help you, but you must take it regularly without fail!" What wise advice that was! And I want to give the same advice to you.

"What aileth thee?" Do not be content with reading Psalm 37 only once or twice; dwell deeply in the promises of God, take regular doses of the medicines He prescribes for you, and you will soon be fit and well, and you will remain fit and well, for His praise and for His glory.

# 6 : Regarding Iniquity in the Heart

*If I regard iniquity in my heart, the Lord will not . . . (Ps. 66: 18)*

Y ou will notice that in quoting Psalm 66: 18, I have omitted the last two words; the whole verse reads: "If I regard iniquity in my heart, the Lord will not hear me." However, I have purposely left out the last two words, because by doing so a very important principle is emphasised. That principle is this: "If I regard iniquity in my heart, the Lord will not . . ."

There are many applications of this principle. One is stated by the psalmist, when he says: ". . . the Lord will not hear me;" but there are other applications of this principle as well. All this means that God is longing to do great things for every one of His children, but whenever and wherever they are consciously harbouring sin, He is hindered from doing so, or, as the writer says, He "will not . . ."

As we progress in the Christian life, and "grow in grace, and in the knowledge of our Lord and Saviour Jesus Christ" (2 Pet. 3: 18), we discover more and more about the sinfulness of our hearts. We more readily agree with the prophet when he says that "the heart is deceitful above all things, and desperately wicked: who can know it?" (Jer. 17: 9); and with the hymnwriter when he says that, "They who fain would serve Thee best are conscious most of wrong within." Our text does not teach us, however, that in this life we shall be completely free from all sin, in every shape and form, that we shall, in fact, reach a state of sinless perfection. This is not taught in scripture, and it is certainly never realised in experience. What our text does, however, is this. It warns us that we may regard, or harbour, sin in our lives, instead of confessing it and forsaking it and seeking God's forgiveness and restoration; and when we do this, our sin creates a barrier between us and God, and it prevents Him from pouring out His blessing upon us and through us. Our sin makes the Lord powerless. He longs to bless, but sin drives a wedge between the soul and God. Sin in the heart and life of the child of God breaks fellowship. Thus, we find that when Isaiah had a vision of the holiness of the Lord, which made him acutely aware of his own sin, he cried out: "Woe is me! for I am undone (or, cut off)" (Isa. 6: 5). Later on, this same servant of God said: "Your iniquities have separated between you and your God, and your sins have hid His face from you" (Isa. 59: 2). Sin separates from God; it erects a barrier between the soul and God, and before we can be in the place of fullness of blessing which God desires for every one of us, it is essential that we deal with sins which are lurking within us, hidden perhaps, but neverthcless sins of which we are conscious and arc secretly holding on to.

The easiest and the most practical way of dealing with this statement made by the psalmist is to unfold the text and take the words as they come. By so doing the significance of each word will be high-lighted.

What docs the first word tell us? It tells us that: (1) *The Christian is under no obligation to sin.* The first little word to notice is the "if". Thank God for that "if"! You see, it implies that we need not sin; we do not have to sin. It is significant to notice that the psalmist says in verse 17: "I cried unto Him with my mouth, and He was extolled with my tongue"; and after speaking as he does in our text, he says: "But verily God hath heard me" (verse 19). So here we have a living illustration of a man who was not regarding sin in his life, and who had learned the secret of victorious living. This must be so, otherwise he could not have said in one statement that if he regarded sin, God would not hear him, and then in the next statement declare that God had heard him!

Many of us long to learn the secret of victorious

Christian living, and if we will study our Bibles, we shall see that through the redemptive and intercessory work of our Lord Jesus Christ, and by the indwelling of the Holy Spirit, God has provided a way of deliverance from sin for every one of His children. In John's first letter, we read: "My little children, these things write I unto you, that ye sin not. And if any man sin, we have an advocate with the Father, Jesus Christ the righteous" (1 John 2: 1). You see, these words clearly tell us that we need not sin; but they also tell us that if, or when, we do sin, we have an advocate, one who represents us and pleads on our behalf in the presence of God. This, of course, is the message of the middle chapters of the Epistle to the Romans; it is summed up in the words of Paul, in Romans 6: 14: "Sin shall not have dominion over you!" God's plan and purpose for you and for me is victory over sin in all its subtle forms and in all its terrible power; but, thank God, victory over sin is provided for every believer!

Now notice the second word: it is the pronoun "I", and this tells us about: (2) *The personal application of this truth.* It is always very important that we do not simply read what the scriptures say. We must apply what we read to our hearts; and surely the personal pronoun here, which indicates that the psalmist was, in fact, giving his testimony, urges us to search and apply this truth to ourselves.

In the opening verses of this Psalm 66, we find that the writer uses the pronouns "we" and "our"; but by the time he reaches the concluding verses, he says "I" and "me" – "If I regard iniquity in my heart . . ."

Do you ever get alone in the presence of God and ask Him to turn the searchlight of His Word upon your life? If you do, you will know what it is to be made conscious of things in your life which are displeasing to the Lord. Do you ever say to yourself: "If I regard iniquity in my heart, the Lord will not . . . For, if I permit sin it will bring a hindrance in my life, for sin breaks fellowship with the Lord"? How very important it is to apply the teaching of the message of our text, not to other people, but to ourselves; to obey the injunction in 1 Corinthians 11: 28: "Let a man examine himself . . ."

Now we come to the third word in our text: it is the word "regard". What does it tell us? It tells us that: (3) *It is possible to harbour sin in the life*. There are a number of dreadful illustrations of this in the Bible; for example, there is the story of Achan, who stole a wedge of gold, a Babylonish garment and some silver, and hid them in his tent (Jos. 7: 21); there is the story of David, who committed adultery with Bathsheba, and in order to hide his sin, sent her husband Uriah into the forefront of the battle so that he might be killed – and he was killed. David then thought that everything would be all right; but the sin was still harboured in his heart (2 Sam. 11: 2–17 and 26–27). In the New Testament we have a more terrible illustration in the case of Ananias and Sapphira. They sold their property for a certain sum of money, and they were under no obligation to give any of it to the Lord's work; but when they brought only a proportion of that amount to the Lord's treasury and deceitfully made out that they were bringing the whole of the purchase price to God, His judgment came down upon them (Acts 5: 1–11).

To "regard iniquity" means to hide the pieces of gold; to "regard iniquity" means to know that we have committed the sin of adultery, or impurity, and to pretend that it did not or does not exist; and to "regard iniquity" means that we go into the presence of God and His people and pretend that we are giving our all to Him, whereas we are, in fact, holding something back from Him. To "regard iniquity", therefore, means to harbour sin; it is to allow it, to gloss it over, to welcome it, to condone it, to excuse it and to be fond of it. Any unconfessed sin of which you and I are conscious in our hearts, in our lives, in our homes, in our business, in our affairs is sin which is "regarded".

Sin that is regarded is sin about which God keeps on

speaking to us; sin that is regarded is sin which comes up before us when we kneel down to pray. What is it that immediately comes into your mind when you kneel down to pray? That is the sin you are regarding. You see, Matthew 5: 23 reads: "If thou bring thy gift to the altar, and there rememberest ..." What is it that you remember? It is that thing that the Lord wants you to confess to, and from which He wants to deliver you, so that you may enter into the experience of 1 John 3: 21: "Beloved, if our heart condemn us not, then have we confidence toward God."

The fourth word in the text is "iniquity". What does this tell us? It tells us that: (4) *The one thing which hinders God's blessing is sin.* What right have we, who belong to the Holy One, to regard iniquity? The scripture says: "Let every one that nameth the Name of Christ depart from iniquity" (2 Tim. 2: 19). This refers to sin in every shape and form. We have no right to have anything to do with that which is unholy and impure. The Lord's word to us is: "Be ye holy; for I am holy" (1 Pet. 1: 16); and His liberating command to us is: "Go, and sin no more" (John 8: 11).

The next word is "heart". What does this tell us? It tells us that: (5) *It is sin in the heart which hinders blessing.* It is sin in the heart which God sees: "Behold, Thou desirest truth in the inward parts" (Ps. 51: 6); that is, in the hidden parts: "For the Lord seeth not as man seeth; for man looketh on the outward appearance, but the Lord looketh on the heart" (1 Sam. 16: 7).

This brings us to the point where we have established the principle that: "If I regard iniquity in my heart, the Lord will not ..." The Lord never glosses over sin. He always judges it and seeks to reveal it to the sinner, so that it may be confessed and put away. His eyes are too pure to behold evil, and He cannot look on iniquity (Hab. 1: 13); and much as He longs to bless, morally He cannot do so, because He cannot bless sin.

Now we need to ask the question: What will the Lord do if I regard iniquity in my heart and life?

## 1. THE LORD WILL NOT HEAR ME

When there is sin in the heart, prayer is vain. This should cause us deep heart-searching, for we must confess that many of us are praying and yet our prayers do not seem to prevail. Why is it that so often we pray and nothing seems to happen? We pray for the salvation of our un-converted loved ones; we pray for revival blessing in our churches; we pray for this, and for that, and somehow so little happens. Why is this? It is because prayer is a mockery unless it is accompanied by a consuming passion to do God's will. The following scriptures make this clear:

What is the hope of the hypocrite . . .? Will God hear his cry? (Job 27: 8–9).

Surely God will not hear vanity, neither will the Almighty regard it (Job 35: 13).

When ye spread forth your hands, I will hide Mine eyes from you: yea, when ye make many prayers, I will not hear . . . Wash you, make you clean; put away the evil of your doings from before Mine eyes; cease to do evil (Isa. 1: 15–16).

Your iniquities have separated between you and your God, and your sins have hid His face from you, that He will not hear (Isa. 59: 2).

Then shall they cry unto the Lord, but He will not hear them . . . as they have behaved themselves ill in their doings (Mic. 3: 4).

They refused to hearken . . . and stopped their ears . . . so they cried, and I would not hear, saith the Lord (Zech. 7: 11–13).

Thus, we see from these scriptures that the truth of

Psalm 66: 18 is clearly stated: that if we regard iniquity in our hearts the Lord will not hear and answer our prayers. But this leads us to a second thing that the Lord will not do if I regard iniquity in my heart and life.

## 2. THE LORD WILL NOT LEAD ME

It is a solemn fact that many of God's children are living self-led, tangled lives; and, of course, it must be so unless God is allowed to have possession of us and guide us in every detail and lead us along the line of His will. But there is only one sure guarantee of a God-guided life, and that is for us to be done with all known sin. It is only as we acknowledge Him in all our ways that He promises to direct our paths (Prov. 3: 6); and it is significant that before the psalmist prays the prayer in Psalm 139: 23–24, "Lead me . . .", he prays, "Search me, O God, and know my heart . . . and see if there be any wicked way in me." If we are out of touch with God, and there is unjudged and unconfessed sin in our lives, we can be quite sure that our fellowship with Him is not what it should be, for sin always breaks fellowship; and where fellowship is broken, we are not open to the Lord's gracious guidance and leading. The great danger is that we shall go before Him, or lag behind Him, and thus get out of His will.

I once heard of a lady who was covered with a mysterious rash which covered her whole body. Despite many visits to the doctor, the trouble did not clear up, and a specialist was called in, but even his efforts failed. Then, one day when her doctor called in to see her, she happened to glance out of the window. Immediately her expression changed, and she said viciously, "That woman next door! I could kill her!" and her whole body shook with passion. Very quietly, the doctor said, "I know now what has caused your rash. You put things right with your neighbour, and then I'll call and see you again!" On his next visit he found that his patient's rash had begun to clear up, and within a few weeks her skin was quite clear again.

We have been thinking about this lady's physical condition, but it may be that you are conscious of some hidden sin in your life; you have a controversy with God, which has created a barrier between you and Him. Maybe it has to do with your relationship with some other Christian – all this is upsetting your physical, your mental and your spiritual life, and God is saying to you, "If you will refuse to regard iniquity any longer, I will lead you into the place of fullness of blessing." What a terrible thing it is for any of us to be out of touch with God, and to allow the rash of unconfessed sin and unadjusted human relationships to mar our lives! This leads us to the third thing that the Lord will not do if I regard iniquity in my heart and life.

### 3. THE LORD WILL NOT USE ME
Is God using you? You can answer this question immediately by a "Yes" or a "No", for the answer does not depend upon the number of people you have had the joy of leading to Christ; it does not depend upon the sermons you have preached. You can answer this question positively or negatively according to whether or not you have dealt faithfully, in the presence of God, with every conscious sin in your life. Of course, God in His sovereign purpose can take and use anyone or anything, but as a spiritual principle, and in relation to the work of His Church and of evangelism, God only uses human channels when they are clean. "In a great house there are not only vessels of gold and of silver, but also of wood and of earth; and some to honour, and some to dishonour. If a man therefore purge himself from these, he shall be a vessel unto honour, sanctified, and meet for the master's use, and prepared unto every good work" (2 Tim. 2: 20–21). In this section of scripture, the apostle Paul makes it perfectly clear that to be available to God for Him to use, we must be purged in order to be a vessel unto honour; we must be sanctified, and made ready for the Master to use. The Lord wants to take and use each one of us, that we may be channels of blessing to others, and that we may bring glory to Him as He uses us as His

instruments. But, when we regard sin in our lives, He cannot do this. He never uses unclean vessels.

How shall we sum up this matter, then? We sum it up and bring it to a conclusion by calling attention to three wonderful verses. They bring us encouragement, hope and the assurance of pardon, cleansing and power.

He that covereth his sins shall not prosper: but whoso confesseth and forsaketh them shall have mercy (Prov. 28: 13).

Having therefore these promises, dearly beloved, let us cleanse ourselves from all filthiness of the flesh and spirit, perfecting holiness in the fear of God (2 Cor. 7: 1).

If we confess our sins, He is faithful and just to forgive us our sins, and to cleanse us from all unrighteousness (1 John 1: 9).

There is a unity about these verses; they all tell us the same thing. Immediately we are made conscious of sin in our hearts or lives, we must confess it and forsake it; we must cleanse ourselves from it, which means, of course, that we must take action; we must repent and turn from sin. Then, and then only, the Lord will forgive us and cleanse us from all unrighteousness.

# 7 : The Full-orbed Christian Life

*I am crucified with Christ: nevertheless I live;*
*yet not I, but Christ liveth in me: and the life*
*which I now live in the flesh I live by the faith*
*of the Son of God, who loved me, and gave*
*Himself for me* (Gal. 2: 20)

What a wonderful verse this is, and what a favourite it is amongst God's people! It is a personal testimony which the apostle Paul wrote to the Church at Galatia; but I would like to underline some of the truths contained in this verse, for of all the statements of texts in the New Testament which describe the Christian life, this is probably the most complete. It describes what we may well call, "The full-orbed Christian life"; and yet it is true to say that to many people it appears to be paradoxical. Here is the testimony of a man who says that he is crucified and dead, and yet the next moment he says that he is alive; and the question arises as to how a man can be dead and alive at the same time! There seems to be a great mystery here.

Of all the translations and paraphrases of this verse which are true to the Greek text, I think I prefer Arthur S. Way's rendering. This is how it reads: "I have shared Messiah's crucifixion. I am living indeed, but it is not I that live; it is Messiah whose life is in me. As for this my earthly existence, I live by virtue of my faith in God's Son, who loved me, and surrendered Himself to death for me."

In unfolding the meaning of this great verse, I want to begin by emphasising several basic truths concerning the Christian life which are clearly stated in it. The first truth to notice is that: (1) *The Christian life is an entirely new life.* It is very important to understand this, for many people believe that the Christian life is the old, unregenerate life improved, patched up or reformed; but the Christian life is an entirely new life which is imparted to us by the Holy Spirit when we believe in the Lord Jesus Christ and are born again, and "except a man be born again, he cannot see the kingdom of God" (John 3: 3). When, through the sovereign work of the Holy Spirit, we become real Christians, the very life of God enters our personalities; we become "partakers of the divine nature" (2 Pet. 1: 4); partakers of the very life of God. If we have become Christians, it is not by virtue of any change in our old life, but it is because we have received a new life through faith in our Lord Jesus Christ; we have "put on Christ" (Gal. 3: 27).

In our text, the apostle Paul speaks of his old life, and he then tells us of the new life he received at his conversion. When he says: "I am (have been) crucified with Christ ..." he is referring to the old life of Saul of Tarsus: to all that he was by nature without Christ, before he became a Christian. When he goes on to say: "nevertheless I live ..." he is referring to the new life which he received from Christ at the time of his conversion on the Damascus road, and which had been his ever since that time. In 2 Corinthians 5: 17, we read: "If any man be in Christ, he is a new creature"; that is, he has become the recipient of a new life altogether; the recipient of eternal life, the Christ-life, the Christian life!

The second truth to notice is that: (2) *The Christian life is a life lived in the flesh.* This means that it is a life lived in the body. Where do you and I have to live the Christian life? In these mortal bodies which God has given us. The word "flesh" is used in two different ways in scripture, and where Paul says: "The life that I now live in the flesh ..." it refers to the sphere in which the believer lives the Christian life, namely, in his physical body. What a wonderful thing it is that in the very sphere in which the first Adam fell, the last Adam, (our Lord Jesus Christ), triumphed so completely: "For as in Adam all die, even so in Christ shall all be made alive" (1 Cor. 15: 22); and through faith in Him, we may also triumph! The sphere in which we are to live the Christian life is not in the clouds, nor in Heaven (just yet!), nor is it in a monastery or a convent; it is in the world, in this earthly body.

The third truth to notice is that: (3) *The Christian life is a life of present victory*. We cannot possibly read Galatians 2: 20 without detecting the great assurance of victory which runs through the whole verse. Read it through, and notice the ring of triumph which sounds through every phrase and word! Get the force of the contrast which Paul makes between his old sinning, failing, unregenerate life, and the new life; "the life which I *now* live . . ." Here is the secret of victorious Christian living. You see, the Christian life is not only a new life given to us by God to live in the flesh, but it is a victorious, triumphant, overcoming, satisfying and God-glorifying life, a life of moment-by-moment victory!

I wonder whether you are enjoying this victorious Christian life, or whether you still need to enter by faith into the full enjoyment of a full-orbed Christian experience?

The fourth truth to notice is that: (4) *The Christian life is a life of faith*. I think I hear someone say, "That is just the problem! That's my difficulty – faith!" No, your problem is unbelief. We all exercise faith all the time. When we buy a return ticket before taking a train journey, we exercise faith that there will be a train to take us to our destination, and when we have fulfilled our purpose in being there, that there will be another train to bring us back home again! We go to church by faith; we read that the service will be held at a certain time, and we go in faith that the service will actually begin at that stated time. We then exercise faith that the pews, or chairs, will support our weight when we sit on them. Our trouble is unbelief; and the writer to the Hebrews warns us against "an evil heart of unbelief" (Heb. 3: 12). But this verse tells us that the Christian life is a life of faith.

What, or who, is the object of our faith? The Son of God, for "the life which I now live in the flesh I live by the faith of (or, by faith in) the Son of God ..." The Christian life, therefore, is a life of faith in the Son of God. What is the simplest definition we can give of faith? Faith is recognising what God says, and reckoning upon it; which means, taking God at His word, believing what He says, and trusting Him. God says a certain thing; I believe Him; I reckon upon that thing; and I trust implicitly in what He says. I rely upon it because God says it.

Now, I want you to notice that in Galatians 2: 20, God says three things about His Son and every believer. A real Christian is a man who believes these three things, and he reckons them to be true because God declares them to be true. What are these three great truths which God declares about His Son and me; about His Son and you; and about His Son and every Christian?

1. HE GAVE HIS LIFE FOR ME

This is the glorious truth which is stated at the end of our text, where we read the words: ". . . the Son of God, who loved me, and gave Himself for me." It is impossible to be a Christian at all and not to believe that. All Christian experience begins when we come to the cross of Calvary as poor, guilty, lost sinners, and recognise in the dying form of the Son of God, our Sinbearer, our Substitute and our Saviour. On the cross, the Lord Jesus died for us; the Just One died for the unjust one (1 Pet. 3: 18); the Guiltless One took the place of the guilty one. Christian experience begins when the Holy Spirit leads us to recognise the truth of the old hymn:

> Bearing shame and scoffing rude,
> In my place condemned He stood;
> Sealed my pardon with His blood:
> Hallelujah! What a Saviour!
>
> *Philip Bliss*

We only begin the Christian life when we are able to make personal that great statement in Isaiah 53: 5: "He was wounded for *my* transgressions, He was bruised for *my* iniquities; the chastisement of *my* peace was upon Him: and with His stripes *I* am healed."

> He knew how sinful I had been,
> He knew that God must punish sin;
> So, out of pity, Jesus said,
> "I'll bear the punishment instead."

Yes, He gave His life for me. That is the first wonderful thing which God says about the Lord Jesus and me; about the Lord Jesus and you; and about the Lord Jesus and every Christian. He gave Himself for us on the cross; and to have faith in the Son of God means, therefore, that we believe this fact, reckon upon it, rely upon it, and rejoice in the wonder of it! Faith cries out: "It is enough that Jesus died, and that He died for me!"

But when the Lord Jesus died upon the cross of Calvary, He not only gave Himself for me, but our text tells us of a second wonderful thing which happened when He died.

## 2. HE TOOK MY LIFE FROM ME

When the apostle Paul said, "I have been crucified with Christ . . ." he was looking right back over the years to the time when the Saviour hung upon the cross, and he was in fact saying, "When He died, I died with Him. In the purpose and intention of God, when the Son of God died, He not only gave Himself for me, but He took my life from me – my old sinful, selfish, unregenerate life which was under the condemnation of God." Here is the great truth of our identification with Christ in His death. Is is judicially true of every believer without exception that he was identified with Christ in His death. God reckons us dead to sin the very moment we put our faith in the Lord Jesus Christ as our personal Saviour. This is not a matter of feeling, but of fact. God says it; therefore it is true. In the reckoning of God, it is just as much a fact that I am dead as that the Lord Jesus was crucified and died on the cross nineteen hundred years ago!

In Romans, chapter 6, this truth is more fully stated. The apostle is writing to believers, and he declares the fact that all believers are already dead through their union with Christ in His death. See what he says:

How shall we, that are *dead* to sin, live any longer therein? Know ye not, that so many of us as were baptised into Jesus Christ were baptised into His *death*? Therefore we are buried with Him by baptism into *death*: that like as Christ was raised up from the dead by the glory of the Father, even so we also should walk in newness of life. For if we have been planted together in the likeness of His *death*, we shall be also in the likeness of His resurrection: knowing this, that *our old man is crucified with Him*, that the body of sin might be destroyed, that henceforth we should not serve sin. For he that is *dead* is freed from sin. Now *if we be dead with Christ*, we believe that we shall also live with Him: knowing that Christ being raised from the dead dieth no more; death hath no more dominion over Him. For in that He died, He died unto sin once: but in that He liveth, He liveth unto God (Rom. 6: 2–10).

Then, notice that in verse 11 we are exhorted: "*Reckon* ye also yourselves to be *dead* indeed unto sin"; in other words, believe God's testimony that when the Lord Jesus died, you died, and reckon upon that.

To reckon that I died with Christ, and that when He died, He took my life from me, is virtually, by faith, to attend my own funeral: and to do this is to enter into God's way of victory, for Romans 6: 7 says: "He that is *dead* is freed from sin." How can a dead man sin? Did you ever know a dead boy to lose his temper? Did you ever hear a dead girl say an unkind word about anyone? Did you ever know a dead man to tell a lie? No: "He that is dead is freed from sin." If, when we are tempted to sin, we reckon ourselves to be "dead indeed unto sin, but alive unto God through Jesus Christ our Lord," we shall experience wonderful deliverance and victory; and this is God's gracious provision for every one of His children.

There is a classic story told concerning George Müller. It is said that on one occasion he was asked the secret of his life, and, speaking very quietly, he said, "A day came in George Müller's experience when George Müller died; and henceforth it was no longer George Müller's desires, George Müller's tastes, George Müller's will, for George Müller was dead!" You and I, in simple faith, may reckon the same thing to be true in our lives.

But there is one more truth enshrined in our text. Not only did the Lord Jesus give His life for me; not only did He take my old life from me, but:

3. HE LIVES HIS LIFE IN ME
The apostle Paul says: "I died with Christ, but now 'Christ liveth in me'."

When Saul of Tarsus met the risen and exalted Lord on the Damascus road, he submitted to Him and acknowledged Him as his Saviour, and the Lord Himself came into Saul's life to live His life in and through Saul's yielded personality. Thank God, not only was this true of Saul of Tarsus, or of Paul, as he afterwards came to be known, but it is true of every Christian! The Lord Jesus lives within us; He indwells us to reproduce His life in us and through us. That, in the simplest possible terms, is what a Christian is: a Christian is *Christ-in*.

This truth of the indwelling presence of Christ in the life of every believer is brought before us in many scriptures. For example: in Philippians 1: 21, we read: "For to me to live is Christ"; in Colossians 1: 27, we read: "Christ in you, the hope of glory"; and in Colossians 3: 4, we read: "Christ, who is our life." Martin Luther once said, "If someone should knock at my heart's door, and ask, 'Who lives here?' I should answer, 'Jesus Christ lives here. Martin Luther used to live here, but he died. Jesus Christ lives here now!' "

What we have to do, therefore, is to believe what God says. We may not fully understand it. Who can? But because God says it, let us lay hold of it; let us reckon upon it. What does He say? He says three wonderful things about the Lord Jesus and me; about the Lord Jesus and you; and about the Lord Jesus and every believer. The first is that when the Lord Jesus died, He died for me; the second is that when the Lord Jesus died, I died with Him; and the third is that when the Lord Jesus died, He rose again and went back to Heaven, and there from the throne of Heaven He imparted His life to me, and now, by the operation and ministry of the Holy Spirit, He lives that life in me and through me.

God says these things, and He waits for us to reckon them to be true. He waits for us to say, "O God, I believe what You say. I believe that the Lord Jesus died for me; I believe also that I died with the Lord Jesus; and I believe that the Lord Jesus now lives His life in me. I take You at Your word, not because I feel it or fully understand it, but because You say it."

May God lead us all into the moment-by-moment, day-by-day experience of this glorious, full-orbed Christian life.

# 8 : Impossible Things made Possible

*The things which are impossible with men are possible with God* (Luke 18: 27)

Things are not always as impossible as they seem! It is true, of course, that there are some situations which are incapable of human solution. To the Christian, however, impossible things become possible; because a Christian is one who has been brought into a special relationship with God as his heavenly Father, and "the things which are impossible with men are possible with God."

It is important to notice that it was the Lord Himself who said that impossible things could become possible; it is also important to remember that the whole Bible is a commentary on these words of our text, and that this truth has been abundantly demonstrated all down the centuries. Best of all, so far as we are concerned, it is being demonstrated today.

You see, it really amounts to this: the God who has revealed Himself to us in His Son Jesus Christ our Lord; the God whom we have been brought to know, is not only all-wise and all-loving, but He is all-powerful: and it is because of this that we are able to prove in our own experience that "the things which are impossible with men are possible with God." In this eighteenth chapter of Luke, a number of things are recorded which illustrate this truth. What are they?

(1) *It is possible for God to answer importunate prayer.*

In verses 1 to 8, we have the record of a parable told by our Lord "to this end, that men ought always to pray, and not to faint." The chief character in the parable is a widow who came to a certain judge, saying, "Avenge me of mine adversary!" He ignored her for a while, but she returned so frequently with the same request that he gave in and acceded to her demand, "lest by her continual coming she weary me ..." Here was someone who prevailed because of her importunity, and the Lord commended her for it; and He gives us very many promises in His Word which assure us that if we will pray, "and not faint", that is, if we will persevere in prayer, then He will hear and answer us. For example, He says: "Verily I say unto you, If ye have faith as a grain of mustard seed, ye shall say unto this mountain, Remove hence to yonder place; and it shall remove; and nothing shall be impossible unto you" (Matt. 17: 20).

When we pray, we "move the hand that rules the universe," so that impossible things become possible. I could write a book containing the factual accounts of answered prayer; not only could I recount incident after incident about which I have heard, over the years, but I could write a whole volume containing the record of my own prayers which God has answered. Some of the things asked for were very "difficult" things, but it is the difficult things which the Lord promises to do. Have you been praying for a long time about a particular matter or a certain person? Do not be discouraged. Have faith in God, for "the things which are impossible with men are possible with God."

(2) *It is possible for God to save the very worst sinners.*

In verses 9 to 14, we read that immediately after narrating the parable of the importunate widow, Jesus told another parable. This concerned a Pharisee and a publican. The Pharisee was religious, but God-less; he could only think of himself and of his "good" acts, and when he prayed, we read that he prayed "with himself", although he addressed himself to God. But the other man, the publican, "standing afar off, would not lift up so much as his eyes unto Heaven, but smote upon his breast, saying, God be merciful to me a sinner." He was a sinner, and he knew it, for what he really said was, "God be merciful to me, *the* sinner." Although he was such a great sinner, he was justified and accepted by God, forgiven

70

and received into His family. We sometimes doubt God's ability to save some people, but however sinful a man may be, the power of God is sufficient to save him, and the blood of Jesus is sufficient to cleanse him, for: "The blood of Jesus Christ His Son cleanseth us from all sin" (1 John 1: 7). Think of Saul of Tarsus, who was "a blasphemer" (1 Tim. 1: 13), but who became one of His most devoted followers. Think of swearing, blaspheming John Newton, who wrote some of our greatest hymns. Think of that loved one of yours, who seems so hard and so far from the Lord, and remember that it is possible for God to save the very worst sinner.

Over the years, I have met many whom the Lord has saved from lives of open sin and rebellion, and I am convinced that He can save the very worst sinners, for:

> Christ receiveth sinful men:
> Even me, with all my sin . . .
> *Erdmann Neumeister*

These words were written in the seventeenth century; but for evidence of the truth that "Christ Jesus came into the world to save sinners" (1 Tim. 1: 15), we need to go right back to the pages of the New Testament, where we read of "the woman who was a sinner" (Luke 7: 37–50); of Zacchaeus (Luke 19: 2–10); and of Mary Magdalene, out of whom the Lord cast seven devils (Luke 8: 2). We can then bring the whole thing up-to-date, for the Lord is doing this today. The most unlikely and unexpected people are being saved through faith in the Lord, for "the things which are impossible with men are possible with God."

(3) *It is possible for God to make Himself known to little children.*

In verses 15 to 17, we have some of the loveliest words in the Bible: "And they brought unto Him (Jesus) also infants, that He would touch them: but when His disciples saw it, they rebuked them. But Jesus called them

71

unto Him, and said, Suffer little children to come unto Me, and forbid them not: for of such is the kingdom of God . . ."

There are some people who do not believe in child conversion, but all the evidence is against them. Samuel was quite young when he came to know the Lord in a most personal way; we do not know his exact age, but he was spoken of as "the child Samuel . . ." when "the Lord revealed Himself" to him (1 Sam. 3: 1 and 21). Many Christians today also testify to the fact that they came to know the Lord when they were quite little children, and I have met many of them; some of them accepted Christ as their Saviour when they were as young as five, six or seven years of age. This should be a very great encouragement to parents and grandparents, and to all who work amongst boys and girls. If a child is old enough to love and hold a conversation with his parents, surely that child is old enough to love the Lord and to hold a conversation with Him.

Let me also take this opportunity of saying here that no one is too old to come to Christ. I have known many people who have turned to Him when they have been in their seventies and eighties, and even later in life, and He has accepted them and given them the assurance of salvation. No one is too young to become a Christian; but no one is too old to find the Lord. If you doubt this, remember that Jesus said: "The things which are impossible with men are possible with God."

(4) *It is possible for God to deliver from the allurements of the world.*

I think we may legitimately make this application from verses 18 to 25, where we read about the rich young ruler. He was religious and had known the commandments from a very early age, and the fact that he came to Jesus indicates that he had a yearning to know more about spiritual things – but he was very rich. Now, there is no sin in being rich; but when riches come before the things of God, then they become sin. Jesus therefore said to him: "Sell all that thou hast, and distribute unto the poor, and thou shalt have treasure in Heaven: and come, follow Me." Alas, the price was too high for the young ruler to pay, and although we read that "he was very sorrowful," he went away. We also read that "when Jesus saw that, He was very sorrowful . . ." and He said: "How hardly shall they that have riches enter into the kingdom of God! For it is easier for a camel to go through the eye of a needle, than for a rich man to enter into the kingdom of God."

What was Jesus referring to when He spoke about "the eye of a needle"? Efforts have been made to refer this to a certain wicket gate through which a camel could pass, but only with extreme difficulty. This could be the right interpretation, but it is more likely that our Lord was referring to an actual needle, with its very small aperture! However, what He was saying was that it is impossible for a rich man to enter the kingdom of God if he holds on to his riches and makes these his god. Anything that we put in the place of God is an idol, and idolatry is sin. Perhaps the reminder we need, if this is our particular sin, is: "The love of money is the root of all evil" (1 Tim. 6: 10). It is certainly not wrong to have riches, but it is wrong to hold on to them and to regard them as exclusively our own. What the Lord asks of us is that we should renounce our possessions; this means that we should take our hands off them and reckon that they belong to the Lord, who has lent them to us, and who has prior claim to them. This is the meaning of Luke 14: 33: "Whosoever he be of you that forsaketh not all that he hath, he cannot be My disciple." To forsake does not necessarily mean that we have to give everything away; it means that we reckon that all our possessions – money, home, car, loved ones etc., are to be used by Him and for Him as He wishes. Let us remember, however, that it is not only rich people who need to be delivered from the allurements of the world. We all need to be delivered from the love of "things": "Love not the world, neither the things that are in the world. If any man love the world, the love of the Father is not in him. For all that is in the world, the lust of the flesh, and the lust of the eyes, and the pride of life, is not of the Father, but is of the world. And the world passeth away, and the lust thereof: but he that doeth the will of God abideth for ever" (1 John 2: 15–17). Can we be delivered from the allurements of the world? Yes, for "the things which are impossible with men are possible with God."

(5) *It is possible for God to compensate us for any sacrifice we may be called upon to make for Him.*

In verses 28 to 30, we read that Peter was concerned about the fact that he and the other disciples had left everything in order to follow Jesus. Would they lose by it? Jesus then gave him some very assuring words: "Verily I say unto you, There is no man that hath left house, or parents, or brethren, or wife, or children, for the kingdom of God's sake, who shall not receive manifold more in this present time, and in the world to come life everlasting."

How we thank God for the many missionaries and Christian workers who have made great sacrifices for the Lord's sake! They have given up home, good prospects, a good salary, and (in some cases) the prospect of marriage, in order that they might be freer and more fitted to proclaim the gospel where the need is greatest. People with a worldly outlook call them "mad"; they join Judas and the other disciples in their criticism of Mary of Bethany, to whom they said, when she gave her most costly possession to the Lord: "To what purpose is this waste?" (Matt. 26: 8) Is it "waste" to give our lives completely and wholeheartedly to the Lord and to His service? See what Jesus had to say about this in verses 29 and 30, which in the parallel passage in Matthew 19: 29 reads like this: "And every one that hath forsaken houses, or brethren, or sisters, or father, or mother, or wife, or children, or lands, for My Name's sake, shall receive an hundredfold, and shall inherit everlasting life." Think of it! "An hundredfold" equals 10,000 per cent. What an investment!

Having said all this, however, we must remember that many Christians who are not in full-time service are called upon to make very great sacrifices for the gospel's sake. Many of them are rarely at home; they seldom enjoy the companionship of their families, and they are constantly having to travel around in order to make Christ known to others. Why do they do it? They do it because the love of Christ constrains them (2 Cor. 5: 14). God will certainly compensate them, if not here and now, then in that day when He will welcome them and say to them: "Well done, thou good and faithful servant: . . . enter thou into the joy of thy Lord" (Matt. 25: 21). Then, if they are asked how they were enabled, joyfully, to make such sacrifices, they will say, "The things which are impossible with men are possible with God."

(6) *It is possible for God to fulfil every promise He has ever made.*

In verses 31 to 34, we read that our Lord told His disciples about His imminent arrest, trial and death upon the cross, and He made it clear to them that all this would take place in fulfilment of the words of the prophets, recorded by them hundreds of years previously. Was He right? Did it happen? Yes, it all came to pass exactly as He had said. This reminds us that every promise and prediction thus far unfulfilled will be fulfilled literally, in God's own time. Some of these prophecies relate to the coming again of Christ, to the rapture of the Church, to the coming of the Son of man in glory, to the time of the Millennium, to the Judgment Seat of Christ, to God's purposes for the Jews and to the judgment of the Great White Throne. All these things may seem impossible of fulfilment, but with God all things are possible.

It seemed an impossible thing to the Virgin Mary that she should be the mother of Jesus, and when the angel Gabriel announced this to her, she expressed her astonishment in the words: "How shall this be, seeing I know not a man?" (Luke 1: 34). However, she believed that this seemingly impossible thing would come to pass, when the angel concluded his message by saying: "For with God nothing shall be impossible" (Luke 1: 26–38).

This is the confidence we need to recapture today. God has made certain great promises concerning His people, concerning the Church, concerning Israel and concerning the world, and: "Hath He said, and shall He not do it?" (Num. 23: 19). Nothing is too hard for the Lord. "Heaven and earth shall pass away, but My words shall not pass away" (Matt. 24: 35). "The things which are impossible with men are possible with God."

(7) *It is possible for God to perform a great miracle.*

In verses 35 to 43, we have the account of the healing of the blind man Bartimaeus. He could see nothing, but at the word of the Lord: "Receive thy sight . . ." we are told: "And immediately he received his sight." Such a thing is quite impossible with man, but not with God.

How impossible it seemed to Abraham and Sarah that they should have a son! They "were old and well stricken in age," but the Lord Himself said: "Is any thing too hard for the Lord?" (Gen. 18: 11 and 14). Abraham was one hundred years old, and was too old to be the father of a child; and Sarah, who was ninety years old, was well past child-bearing; yet they were "strong in faith . . . being fully persuaded that, what He had promised, He was able also to perform" (Rom. 4: 18–21). The impossible thing became possible – and actual. So Abraham and Sarah proved that nothing was too hard for the Lord.

Is anything too hard for the Lord? Are there some situations which are too difficult for Him to sort out? Are there some problems which He cannot solve? Are there any sinners He is unable to save? Is there a backslider anywhere whom He cannot restore? Is there a church which He cannot revive?

Perhaps you are facing some very trying situation, some problem which is so great that you feel it cannot ever be solved. Humanly speaking, there does not seem to be a way out; but why use the words "humanly speaking"? Bring God into the picture and relate your situation to Him. He will see you through! for "the things which are impossible with men are possible with God."

Before leaving this eighteenth chapter of Luke, I would like to ask this question: How big is your God? How big is my God? In other words, do we sufficiently recognise His greatness and His power? If we do, surely we shall come to Him and prove for ourselves that "the things which are impossible with men are possible with God."

Got any rivers you think are uncrossable?
Got any mountains you can't tunnel through?
God specialises in things thought impossible,
He does the things which no others can do.

# 9 : Every Christian's Greatest Need

*Now when all the people were baptised, it
came to pass, that Jesus also being baptised,
and praying, the heaven was opened. And the
Holy Ghost descended in a bodily shape like a
dove upon Him, and a voice came from
Heaven, which said, Thou art My beloved
Son; in Thee I am well pleased* (Luke 3:21–22)

When the Lord Jesus was baptised by John the Baptist, at the commencement of His public ministry,
the Holy Ghost descended in a bodily shape like a dove
upon Him; and there is no greater need in your life or in
mine than that the same Holy Spirit should come upon
us like a dove. Before we can ever live victoriously or
serve effectively, before we can ever be the men and women
God would have us to be, we must experience this holy
anointing. Indeed, it is not too much to say that the reason
for all our failure in Christian living and our fruitlessness
in Christian service may be traced to the fact that so often
we try to live for the Lord and to serve Him without
receiving this anointing of the Holy Spirit. This is our
greatest need. It is the great imperative.

Now, the Lord Jesus was conceived of the Holy Spirit:
"The angel of the Lord appeared unto him in a dream,
saying, Joseph . . . fear not to take unto thee Mary thy
wife: for that which is conceived in her is of the Holy
Ghost" (Matt. 1: 20). He was born of the Holy Spirit:
"The Holy Ghost shall come upon thee, and the power of
the Highest shall overshadow thee: therefore also that
holy thing which shall be born of thee shall be called the
Son of God" (Luke 1: 35). He lived a perfect, holy,
sinless life: "For such an high priest became us, who is
holy, harmless, undefiled, separate from sinners . . ."
(Heb. 7: 26). He came into the world, gladly and voluntarily, to save sinners: "Christ Jesus came into the world

78

to save sinners . . ." (1 Tim. 1: 15). But before our Lord Jesus Christ could begin that work for which He had come, He needed this holy anointing, this mighty endurement with power; and at His baptism, while He stood in Jordan's water and prayed, the Holy Ghost descended in a bodily shape like a dove upon Him. Afterwards, in the synagogue at Nazareth, He was able to say: "The Spirit of the Lord is upon Me, because He hath anointed Me to preach the gospel . . ." (Luke 3: 18); and later, Peter was able to say: "God anointed Jesus of Nazareth with the Holy Ghost and with power" (Acts 10: 38).

For the Lord Jesus, the blessed Son of God, our Saviour, this was a definite experience, a holy anointing. There was a "before" and an "after". There was a time before when this anointing was not His; and ever after, during those three years of public ministry, this holy, blessed anointing was resting upon Him. But this experience was not only for the Saviour; it was also for His first followers, for in this same chapter we read: "John answered, saying unto them all, I indeed baptise you with water; but One mightier than I cometh, the latchet of whose shoes I am not worthy to unloose: He shall baptise you with the Holy Ghost . . ." (Luke 3: 16). You will remember, too, that before His ascension, the Lord Jesus said to His disciples: "Tarry ye in the city of Jerusalem, until ye be endued with power from on high . . . Ye shall receive power, after that the Holy Ghost is come upon you" (Luke 24: 49; Acts 1: 8). Then, shortly after this promise had been given by the Lord, it was fulfilled, for "when the day of Pentecost was fully come, they were all with one accord in one place . . . and they were all filled with the Holy Ghost" (Acts 2: 1 and 4).

But we must not stop there – in the Book of Acts! What about ourselves? For this blessed, life-transforming, service-empowering anointing was not only for the Lord Jesus; it was not only for those first disciples and followers of His; it is for every one of us, for every Christian, everywhere. This is the indispensable qualification for holy, effective living and service. This is the greatest need today in the Christian Church. This is our greatest need.

This is a great mystery, that our Lord Jesus Christ, who was holy, harmless, undefiled and separate from sinners, should need this great qualification before He could enter upon His public ministry. There is no mystery about the fact that the disciples needed and received this anointing, for what a transformation was wrought in them and through them! But we, too, before we can live for the Lord as He would have us live, and before we can serve Him effectively, must know what it is for the same blessed Holy Spirit to come upon us like a dove.

Why did the Holy Spirit descend upon our Lord "in a bodily shape like a dove"? This surely is significant. I think it is because the dove is noted for four qualities: purity, beauty, humility and alacrity. Purity: in the Song of Solomon 6: 9, the bridegroom is speaking to the bride, and he calls her, "my dove, my undefiled". Beauty: in Psalm 68: 13 we read, "Though ye have lien among the pots, yet shall ye be as the wings of a dove covered with silver, and her feathers with yellow gold." Humility: in Matthew 10: 16, it is recorded that our Lord said, "Be ye harmless as doves." Alacrity: in Psalm 55: 6, the writer cries out, "Oh that I had wings like a dove!" Purity, beauty, alacrity.

In the case of our Lord Jesus Christ, the Holy Spirit came upon Him and endued Him with power like a dove because He already possessed these dove-like qualities. He already possessed in perfection – purity, beauty, humility, and alacrity to do God's will. The Holy Ghost came upon Him as a seal from Heaven, because here all these graces and virtues were seen in absolute perfection. But in our case, because we are sinful beings and are so unlike our Lord, the Holy Ghost comes upon us like a dove to impart these qualities of purity, beauty, humility and alacrity. Jesus was already pure and beautiful in His life, and He was humble and ready to do God's will with alacrity in ever respect; but you and I need the Holy Ghost to make us pure, to make us beautiful, to bring us down in the place of humble submission to the will of God, and to make us alert always to do His will.

Thomas Goodwin, a great old writer, said: "All apparitions of God at any time, made of Himself, were made to men, not so much to show what God is in Himself, as to declare what effects He will work in us." So when the Holy Ghost came upon the Lord Jesus as a dove, it was not so much to declare the purity, the beauty, the humility and the alacrity of the Lord Himself, but to show that these qualities would afterwards be imparted to us by the Person, the presence and the power of the Holy Ghost. In other words, the Holy Ghost comes like a dove in order to show us that He would make us dove-like. Now, let us see what this means when He comes upon us in His anointing power.

(1) *When the Holy Spirit comes upon us "like a dove"*, WE SHALL KNOW HIS PURITY.

In other words, He will purify our lives. Whatever theories we may have concerning the Pentecostal blessing, we simply cannot evade the fact that when the Holy Ghost came upon the early Christians, they were purified. We sometimes sing the words of Charles Wesley:

> Oh, that in me the sacred fire
>     Might now begin to glow;
> Burn up the dross of base desire,
>     And make the mountains flow.

> Thou, who at Pentecost didst fall,
>     Do Thou my sins consume;
> Come, Holy Ghost, for Thee I call;
>     Spirit of burning, come.

> Refining fire, go through my heart,
>     Illuminate my soul;
> Scatter Thy life through every part,
>     And sanctify the whole.

And so I repeat that the first thing we shall know, when the Holy Ghost comes upon us like a dove, is His purity. Jesus said, "Ye shall receive power, after that the Holy Ghost is come upon you . . ." (Acts 1: 8); and when that power came on the day of Pentecost, there was a deep inward cleansing and purifying. How carnal these Christians were! How full of dreadful failure they were – until the day of Pentecost! Then a change was seen in them. The impurity of pride, jealousy, sectarianism, vindictiveness, and even envy and criticism was among them; but when the Holy Ghost came upon them like a dove, there was a deep inward cleansing.

> O Spirit of faith and love,
>    Work in our midst, we pray,
> And purify each waiting heart . . .
> *H. E. Blair*

This is our great need. Do we not need to be cleansed from these impurities? Do we not long to be free from them? What is the way? The Holy Ghost must come upon us like a dove; and if He were to come down upon us, we should have this dove-like quality of inward heart-purity, and we should have power to live radiant lives and power to serve Him as He wants.

Someone who has been greatly used of God once gave a testimony which was made a great blessing to me. He said, "For years I prayed for power, but one day God showed me that what I needed to pray for first of all was purity." Is that a word for you? How can we know this purity? The Holy Ghost must come upon us like a dove.

(2) *When the Holy Spirit comes upon us "like a dove"*, WE SHALL REFLECT HIS BEAUTY.

In other words, He will beautify our lives. He will answer the prayer which we so often sing:

> Let the beauty of Jesus be seen in me,
> All His wondrous compassion and purity:

>Oh, Thou Spirit divine,
>All my nature refine,
>Till the beauty of Jesus be seen in me.

That is the only possible way for the beauty of the Lord Jesus to be really adequately reflected in our lives. It can never be achieved by striving or by external things. This is God's purpose in saving us: "He will beautify the meek with salvation" (Ps. 149: 4).

Stephen, the first Christian martyr, was a mighty man of God; but the time came when he was apprehended and brought before the Jewish leaders for trial. As he made his defence, we read that "all that sat in the council, looking steadfastly on him, saw his face as it had been the face of an angel" (Acts 6: 15). What is the explanation of this? It is that he was filled with the Holy Spirit (Acts 6: 5 and 7: 55); he knew what it was for the Holy Ghost to come upon him like a dove. The same thing was true of Peter and John. When the Jewish leaders looked at them, they were at once impressed with the fact that "they had been with Jesus" (Acts 4: 13); they were like their Lord; and when the Holy Ghost comes upon us like a dove, we too shall know His purity, and we shall reflect His beauty. "Let the beauty of the Lord our God be upon us . . ." (Ps. 90: 17).

(3) *When the Holy Spirit comes upon us "like a dove"*, WE SHALL SHARE HIS HUMILITY.

In other words, He will make us "meek and lowly in heart", as He was (Matt. 11: 29). There is something deeply humbling about this. How gentle the Lord Jesus was! and how gentle the "rough and ready" disciples became under the anointing of the Spirit of God!

In his book, *Emblems of the Holy Spirit,* Dr F. E. Marsh says that one reason that is given for the gentleness of the dove is that the bird has no gall, which according to the naturalists of old, is the fountain of contention, the bitterness of the gall being supposed to infuse itself into the spirit. So here we have a contrast: the gall of pride and contention and bitterness, and the dove of gentleness and meekness and humility.

It is unfortunately true that often our lives are spoiled by the gall of pride; often they are lacking in humility. When I was in India, I overheard one missionary say to another: "I apologise for saying that the other day. I ought not to have said it!" That was a mark of humility. Then I knew a man who attended some Convention meetings, as the result of which he wrote a letter to someone because God had put His finger upon something in his life. He wrote the letter to apologise for his critical and careless talk. That was a mark of humility. On the other hand, I know of another man who went to a fellow Christian, and said, "I demand an apology!" That was a mark of pride; that was the gall of bitterness and contention.

Jesus said: "Learn of Me; for I am meek and lowly in heart . . ." (Matt. 11: 29). He was meek, but He was not weak; and the message He was trying to get across to His disciples was that if they were going to be His followers they would have to share His humility. How? When the Holy Ghost comes upon a man like a dove, there is no gall of contention or pride in that person. When He comes, we are made gentle, loving, meek and easy to live with; in a word, we are made Christ-like. A lady once spoke to me concerning her husband, and she commented: "You know, he's not very good in the morning!" We know what she meant! How can this weakness be dealt with? Well, it can be when the Holy Ghost comes upon us like a dove.

(4) *When the Holy Spirit comes upon us "like a dove"*, WE SHALL EXPERIENCE HIS ALACRITY.

In other words, He will make us quick and eager to do His bidding. The meaning of this word "alacrity" is described in my dictionary as: "readiness, eagerness, gladness, promptitude". In what way does the Holy Spirit impart this dove-like quality? He makes us eager and ready to do the will of God; swift to obey God's bidding;

and He gives us a longing to do what God wants. Away back in eternity, Jesus said: "Lo, I come: in the volume of the book it is written of Me, I delight to do Thy will, O My God: yea, Thy law is within My heart" (Ps. 40: 7–8). Do you feel like that? Do you want to do the will of the Lord with alacrity? But how can we do that? When the Holy Ghost comes upon us like a dove, He puts within us a burning desire to do the will of God, to be in the place of His choice, and from our hearts there bursts forth a prayer: "Thy will be done in my life, O God – at all costs!"

In Acts 8: 26, we read that the Lord said to Philip: "Arise, and go . . ."; and in the next verse we are told: "He arose and went." Then, in verse 29, the Holy Spirit said to him: "Go near, and join thyself to this chariot"; and the next verse says: "Philip ran . . ." That is what I mean by alacrity. How eager this man was to obey God! What was the secret? The Holy Ghost had come upon him like a dove; he was filled with the Spirit (Acts 6: 3 and 5).

We must conclude by asking: What, then, must we do if we would be anointed with the Holy Spirit, and thus fitted to live for God's glory and to serve Him, not in the energy of the flesh, but "in demonstration of the Spirit and of power" (1 Cor. 2: 4)? What is the secret of this Spirit-anointed life? It is a two-fold secret, which is seen in the experience of our Lord. His baptism was the indication, the token, that He was utterly abandoned to the will of His Father. He was unreservedly at God's disposal for His will to be done, which in our Lord's case was the accomplishing of the work of redemption. He was in effect saying: "Here I am, O Father; it is for this purpose that I came into the world. I have come to do Thy will."

But we are told something else: this is the second part of the secret. As He stood in Jordan's waters, Luke tells us that it was while He prayed that the anointing came upon Him: "Jesus also being baptised, and praying, the heaven was opened, and the Holy Ghost descended in a bodily shape like a dove upon Him ..." (Luke 3: 21–22). You see, prayer always precedes the coming of the Holy Ghost in power. Prayer preceded Pentecost, and it was the same after Pentecost, for: "when they had prayed, the place was shaken ..." (Acts 4: 31). It was the same in the case of Saul of Tarsus. The Lord commissioned Ananias to go and seek Saul in Damascus, "for, behold, he prayeth" (Acts 9: 11); and when Ananias went to this new convert and laid his hand upon him, the Holy Ghost came upon him like a dove (Acts 9: 17–18), and he went out to live and to labour for his Lord in mighty power and blessing.

If you would know the Holy Ghost coming upon you like a dove, you must make sure that your life is fully given over to the Lord, and that you desire above everything else to be in the centre of God's will; then you must get alone in the place of prayer, and wait there until God meets with you. There is no need for you to wait *for* God, but there is need for you to wait *upon* God. God is longing to meet with you; and when the Holy Ghost comes upon you like a dove, you will have His purity, His beauty, His humility and His alacrity.

See the Lord Jesus standing there in Jordan's waters – praying, and saying, in effect: "Here I am; Thy will be done." As He does so, suddenly the Holy Ghost descends in a bodily shape like a dove upon Him. And, as you see Him there, hear Him say to you: "As My Father hath sent Me, even so send I you ... Receive ye the Holy Ghost" (John 20: 21–22).

This blessed experience of the Holy Spirit's anointing can be ours; indeed, it must be our experience if ever we are to be the men and women God would have us be. This is, therefore, our greatest need. This is every Christian's greatest need.

# 10 : Living with the End in View

*The end of all things is at hand . . . (1 Pet. 4: 7)*

We must be careful to study these words, "the end of all things is at hand", against the background of 1 Peter 4: 7–11. The apostle Peter was writing to encourage Christians who were living in a time of crisis; and this makes the theme of this message particularly relevant, for we are living in a time of crisis and we need encouragement.

But what did Peter mean when he said, "The end of all things is at hand"? He may have referred to the impending end of the old Jewish economy; or he may have had in mind the approaching end of life itself, for many Christians were being martyred and were laying down their lives for Christ's sake, as we learn from 1 Peter 4: 12: "Beloved, think it not strange concerning the fiery trial which is to try you . . ." There is, however, something more than this suggested here: I believe Peter was making reference to the end of the age, to the second advent, to the coming again of Christ. All the early Christians believed in and expected the Lord's return; and we today are to live with this end in view; we are to live in the light of the fact that Jesus is coming again, and to remember that "the coming of the Lord draweth nigh" (Jas. 5: 8) – the time is short! If we live in the light of this, it will affect our living, our praying, our loving and our serving, for in the New Testament the truth of the second advent is always presented as a very practical matter which affects character and service. What difference will it make to us if we live with the end in view? Peter tells us in this portion of scripture – 1 Peter 4: 7–11.

(1) *If we believe that the time is short, that Jesus is soon coming, we shall live a calm and an ordered life.*

The apostle Peter wrote: "The end of all things is at

hand: be ye therefore sober, and watch unto prayer" (verse 7); and by this he meant, live a calm and an ordered life. Notice that he did not only write, "Be sober ..." but, "be ye therefore sober ..." In other words, because the end is in view, "keep sound-minded"; or, as another rendering has it, "lead an ordered and a quiet life." The early Christians needed this exhortation, for they were surrounded by those who were godless and very antagonistic to all who claimed allegiance to our Lord Jesus Christ. We need the same exhortation today, for we are living in a world which has no time for God, and we need to be kept from being dragged down to the level of the pagan society around us. We need also to experience calmness and confidence as we hear of "wars and rumours of wars" (Matt. 24: 6), so that instead of being filled with alarm and panic, we are kept "in perfect peace" (Isa. 26: 3).

In the early part of the 1939–1945 War, I received an invitation to my first pastorate, which was on the Kent coast, and was in those days considered to be a "danger" zone. When we arrived at our new home, we found that several of our neighbours were in process of moving out of the district; in fact, it was a common sight to walk down almost any road and see a furniture van loading up with furniture and household goods. Everyone was moving to a "safe" area, and as the threat of invasion was a very real one, we could not blame them. I must confess to a measure of alarm at the prospect of being left behind! Then, one day I noticed that two of our new friends over the road had placed a text in their window. It was from Proverbs 1: 33: 'Whoso hearkeneth unto Me shall dwell safely, and shall be quiet from fear of evil." This had a profound effect on me. We did not know what the night, or the next day, might bring, but from that moment on I knew what it was to "be quiet from fear of evil". This is what Peter is saying here; and what a word this is for today! Why worry and be alarmed, when the next great event may be the return of the Lord?

(2) *If we believe that the time is short, that Jesus is soon coming, we shall be men and women of prayer.*

In verse 7, Peter goes on to urge his readers to "watch unto prayer". The word "watch" suggests exercising oneself in prayer and guarding against drowsiness or slackness. We are to do this, not for the benefit which we shall receive ourselves, but for the benefit our prayers will bestow upon others. There is, of course, always a reflex result when we pray, for in praying down blessings upon others, we are wonderfully enriched ourselves. We have an illustration of this in Job 42: 10: "The Lord turned the captivity of Job, when he prayed for his friends: also the Lord gave Job twice as much as he had before."

The philosophy of prayer is hard to understand. If God wants to bless us, why do we need to pray? The answer is that He has ordained it this way. In Ezekiel 36: 37 we read: "Thus saith the Lord God; I will yet for this be inquired of by the house of Israel, to do it for them . . ." There are some things which God will do if we pray, which He will not do if we fail to pray. Therefore, with vigilance and diligence we are to "watch unto prayer". We are to pray alone; we are to pray constantly: "Praying always with all prayer and supplication in the Spirit, and watching thereunto with all perseverance and supplication . . ." (Eph. 6: 18).

When we remember all that prayer can accomplish, it is certainly an amazing thing that we do not pray more often and more expectantly. Have you ever noticed in the Bible the many promises which God makes to those who will pray, and the illustrations which are recorded there of men and women who prayed and had their prayers answered? How strange it is that we do not make more use of prayer! Even God is amazed when His people do not pray, for in Isaiah 59: 16 we read: "He saw that there was no man, and wondered that there was no intercessor . . ." So much can be accomplished by the prayers of one Christian, for "the effectual fervent prayer of a righteous man availeth much" (Jas. 5: 16). How much? Most of us still have to find this out for ourselves! Many of us could fill a book with the details of prayers which we, or our friends, have offered, and which in response to these prayers, God has abundantly answered; but for all that, we do not pray enough. Surely the imminence of the Saviour's return should spur us on to pray.

(3) *If we believe that the time is short, that Jesus is soon coming, we shall love one another fervently.*

Notice the challenge in verse 8 of this chapter: "And above all things have fervent charity among yourselves: for charity shall cover the multitude of sins." We are to be loving, and here we are told that we are to be loving "above all things", and our loving is to be "fervent"; this love is to be experienced "among (y)ourselves", or, as it might read: "Do not let your love for one another flag or diminish." Why are we to love like this? One reason is given: "For love covers . . ." Whose sins does love cover? Our sins, or the other person's? It means that love will always find a way to forgive and forget.

One of the most challenging things that Jesus ever said is recorded in Matthew 18: 21–22: "Then came Peter to Him, and said, Lord, how oft shall my brother sin against me, and I forgive him? till seven times? Jesus saith unto him, I say not unto thee, Until seven times: but, Until seventy times seven." But how is this possible? How can we love one another fervently? Peter tells us why we need to love one another in this way: he says, ". . . for charity shall cover the multitude of sins" (verse 8). This means that as we love, we shall manifest the fruit of the Spirit in our lives, and this is: "love, joy, peace, longsuffering, gentleness, goodness, faith . . ." (Gal. 5: 22).

On one occasion I preached about the need for Christians to love one another. Afterwards, a friend came to me and said, "It's quite impossible for me to love my son-in-law! He's unreasonable, he's difficult, he's – well, I just can't love him!" I answered her something like this: "Well, you're obviously quite right. You can't love him! Why, you haven't enough love to love him!" She looked startled, but she said, "So it's all right if I don't love him?" "No," I replied, "it's all wrong! You must love him, and you can love him, but not with your own love; you can only love him with God's love. You are a Christian, and therefore, according to Romans 5: 5, the love of God is shed abroad in your heart; so you can love him, but not with your own love; you can love him with the love which is 'the fruit of the spirit'." That is the only way to love others; and with God's love filling our hearts we can love everyone with fervent love.

(4) *If we believe that the time is short, that Jesus is soon coming, we shall set out to be friendly.*

This is the deeper meaning of verse 9: "Use hospitality one to another without grudging." The reference here is to opening our homes to friends and strangers. This was a very necessary ministry in the first century; but there is still a great work to be carried on along this line today. Many Christians have opened their homes to those who are lonely and subject to attacks of depression and fear, and they have been the means of bringing joy and encouragement into these lives. With all the rush and hurry of our modern way of life, it is easy to forget the many whose lives are drab and dull because they feel friendless and unwanted.

But there is another way in which we can exercise a most valuable ministry by opening up our homes. Have you ever thought of being a spiritual foster parent to a new convert? How I thank God for two people who helped me soon after I became a Christian! One of them invited me to tea on Sunday afternoons, and then he took me to services in churches and chapels in and around London where he was to preach. He was a spiritual father to me, and I can never be thankful enough for what I learned of the Lord and of the Christian life, both in his home and in his preaching. This is a ministry in which many can engage. It is a tragedy for a Christian to possess a lovely home, and yet to be self-centred and inward looking, when all the time there are young believers needing to be encouraged and nurtured in the things of

God, and there are those who are without Christ who need to be "loved" into His kingdom. Why not open your home to Christians who are young believers, or to those who are away from home and needing your friendship and love? If you do this, you may well find that you are entertaining angels unawares! (Heb. 13: 2).

The root meaning of the word "hospitality", as it is used here, has to do with friendliness, not just in the home, but in the heart. This is one way in which the love of verse 8 will express itself. In our churches and assemblies there is a great need for friendliness, and when our hearts are filled with love and compassion, we shall want to express that love and compassion in the care of others.

(5) *If we believe that the time is short, that Jesus is soon coming, we shall be busy in the Lord's work.*

In verse 10, we are reminded that God has entrusted to us all some spiritual gift, or gifts, which we must exercise for the benefit of the saints: "As every man hath received the gift, even so minister the same one to another, as good stewards of the manifold grace of God." The Holy Spirit has imparted some special "divine endowment" to every believer. We are trustees of the gifts of the Spirit, and we must use them, especially as we live in anticipation of the Lord's return. Our Lord reminded us about this privilege and responsibility: "He said therefore, A certain nobleman went into a far country to receive for himself a kingdom, and to return. And he called his ten servants, and delivered them ten pounds, and said unto them, Occupy till I come . . ." (Luke 19: 12–13).

One of the greatest needs in our churches and assemblies today is for workers, for many church members, alas, are like those described in Amos 6: 1: "Woe to them that are at ease in Zion . . ."; and in Judges 5: 23: "Curse ye Meroz, saith the angel of the Lord, curse ye bitterly the inhabitants thereof; because they came not to the help of the Lord, to the help of the Lord against the mighty." Many people are very enthusiastic about their hobbies, their sport or their favourite pastime; others give themselves wholeheartedly to the advancement of their political party, or the increase in the turnover of their business; and many, who are caught up with false teaching and are associated with one or another of the many cults, are very busy propagating their dangerous doctrines. What the Church of Jesus Christ needs is men and women who are utterly dedicated to the Lord and who will give themselves wholeheartedly to Him to use as He wishes. There are vacancies for workers in every church, in every missionary society and in every sphere of Christian work; and if we are available to Him, the Lord will give us all the ability that we need to carry out His work for His glory. Is it possible that we are shirkers instead of being workers?

(6) *If we believe that the time is short, that Jesus is soon coming, we shall speak boldly in His Name.*

In verse 11, we read: "If any man speak, let him speak as the oracles of God; if any man minister, let him do it as of the ability which God giveth ..." This means that we are each to be "a mouthpiece of God", and that we should speak for Him "with ability which He gives"; that is, we should speak not in our own strength but in His strength and with the enabling of the Holy Spirit.

Christians frequently say, "I can't speak for the Lord!" We say we are willing to live for Him, and perhaps to work for Him, but when it comes to speaking for Him, well, we are not able to do that! This is exactly what Jeremiah said; but the Lord said to him: "Behold, I have put My words in thy mouth" (Jer. 1: 9). Jeremiah trusted the Lord, and God used him mightily; and if we will trust Him to give us His words to speak, He will do just that.

All around us there are souls who need to be told about the Saviour. Who will speak to them if we do not? The rapid progress and growth of the early Church was due, under the blessing of the Holy Spirit, to the determined effort of the early Christians to make Christ known. Even when they were forbidden to speak of Him, they continued to do so, simply because they could not help it! "Peter and John answered and said unto them, Whether it be right in the sight of God to hearken unto you more than unto God, judge ye. For we cannot but speak the things which we have seen and heard" (Acts 4: 19–20). There would be a mighty revival if all who name the Name of Christ would begin to speak about Him to their relatives and friends. What excuse have we for not doing so? Are we so selfish that we are willing to be saved ourselves and let our loved ones, friends and neighbours go to Hell? Surely not!

In 2 Kings 7: 1–11, we read of four leprous, starving men outside the city of Samaria. Suddenly they came upon the spoil which had been left behind by the Syrians who had been besieging the city. There, before their eyes were food, clothing, money . . . It was unbelievable! They fell upon it, and began to devour what they could and at the same time began to put things on one side for themselves; but in the midst of their enjoyment they remembered the starving people in the city, and they said: "We do not well: this day is a day of good tidings, and we hold our peace: . . . now therefore come, that we may go and tell the king's household!" And they returned to the city and shared the good news; and they were in time to save many from death.

(7) *If we believe that the time is short, that Jesus is soon coming, we shall do everything to the glory of God.*

Verse 11 concludes with some very wonderful words: "That God in all things may be glorified through Jesus Christ, to whom be praise and dominion for ever and ever. Amen"; and it is helpful to compare these words with 1 Corinthians 10: 31, where the apostle Paul says: "Whether therefore ye eat, or drink, or whatsoever ye do, do all to the glory of God."

What does it mean to do everything to the glory of God? It means that we shall seek, with God's enabling, to think, speak and act only in ways which are pleasing to

Him and which honour His Name. We have a good illustration of this in Colossians 3: 17, where Paul, writing to the Christians at Colosse, says: "Whatsoever ye do in word or deed, do all in the Name of the Lord Jesus, giving thanks to God and the Father by Him." He sets this exhortation in the context of daily living in the home, in the church and in all the relationships of life. How God would be honoured were we always to take heed to these exhortations!

A few years ago we had a calendar sent to us for Christmas. On it were two words – *Perhaps Today*! That is the message Peter wanted to get across in this section of scripture we have been considering. That is the message which we need to hear, and to keep on hearing day by day.

Recordings of these sermon-studies, as originally given, are available on standard tapes and cassettes from WORDS OF LIFE MINISTRIES, 4/5 Regency Mews, Silverdale Road, Eastbourne, BN20 7AB, England.